Gathering

*A search for
balance and
fulfillment*

*Sandra Finley Doran &
Dale Finley Slongwhite*

Pacific Press® Publishing Association
Nampa, Idaho
Oshawa, Ontario, Canada

Edited by Jerry D. Thomas
Designed by Tim Larson
Cover art by Hermann Seeger (1857-1920)
On the Beach
© CHRISTIE'S IMAGES

Doran, Sandra Finley, 1954-
    Gathering : a search for balance and fulfillment / Sandra
Doran, Dale Finley Slongwhite
        p.   cm.
    ISBN 0-8163-1696-1 (pbk.)
    1. Doran, Sandra Finley, 1954-   . 2. Slongwhite, Dale
Finley, 1951-   . 3. Seventh-Day Adventists—United States—
Biography.
I. Slongwhite, Dale Finley, 1951-   . II. Title.
BX6191.D67A3   1999
286' . 732'092273—dc21
[B]   98-50106
                                                            CIP

99 00 01 02 03 • 5 4 3 2 1

DEDICATED TO

My sons,
Eric and Jeff
(Sandra)

and to

My daughters,
Karen and Laurel
(Dale)

As you gather your lives.

TABLE OF
CONTENTS

A Horizontal Gathering	Sandra	7
Gathering Insight	Dale	13
Gathering Strength	Sandra	21
Gathering Moments	Dale	25
Gathering Mercy	Sandra	31
Gathering Truth	Dale	35
Gathering Richness	Sandra	39
Gathering Common Bonds	Dale	43
Gathering Up the Pieces	Sandra	49
Gathering Knowledge	Dale	53
Gathering Courage	Sandra	59
Gathering Rituals	Dale	63
Gathering New Angles	Sandra	67
Gathering Thankfulness	Dale	71
Gathering Rays	Sandra	77
Gathering Silver	Dale	81
Gathering Hope	Sandra	85
Gathering Friends	Dale	89
Gathering Perspective	Sandra	95
Gathering Identity	Dale	99
Gathering Wins and Losses	Sandra	103
Gathering Light	Dale	109
Gathering the Unexpected	Sandra	113

Gathering Possibilities   Dale   119
Gathering Awareness   Sandra   125
Gathering the Bounty   Dale   129
Gathering a Family   Sandra   135
Gathering Warmth   Dale   143
Gathering Still   Sandra   149
Gathering a Sense of Place   Dale   155

A HORIZONTAL

Gathering

Sandra Doran

"No place, no profession, in itself can effectuate a life;
it is the individual perception, the insight, the grasp,
the quality of the ecstasy and the pain that make it whole,
that fill the cup." —Agnes Sligh Turnbull, The Golden Journey.

The young woman looked at me expectantly. "Is there anything else you would like to add?" she asked.

I scanned the paragraph she had put together for the conference bulletin. "Sandra Doran is a career woman . . ." it began.

I flinched, acutely aware that the task of condensing my life into one paragraph was not easy. But somehow, "career woman" seemed to say things that were different from the way I saw my own life. Reflecting for a moment, I tried to describe the difference. Yes, I was employed in a professional position. Yes, I found satisfaction and fulfillment by engaging in meaningful work. But it was just that the term sounded so limiting . . . so *vertical*, I decided. One could almost visualize a woman in high heels climbing a ladder, her dark-clad form shrinking in size as she reached higher and higher levels. Somehow the picture didn't match the way I lived my life. For me, work was part of a much larger picture, a blending of talent and place, another way to express myself in that time and place. My life, I decided, was not so much a *vertical climb* as a *horizontal gathering*.

I turned to the young woman. "I earned a doctorate while passing through a church district once," I said. Her confused look told me I had a long way to go.

Since earning a bachelor's degree more than twenty years ago, I have sought not so much to build a career, but a life—choosing to work full time, part time, or not at all, depending on my current situation. Newly married with teaching credentials in hand, I commuted thirty miles to a small school each day, toting a box of student papers, books, paints, math cubes, and dreams while my husband finished his theology degree. Later, 1,000 miles away on a university campus while Eric pursued a master of divinity degree, I reached out on a wild whim and secured my first job as a writer. I interviewed faculty, staff, and students and left at the end of the day with nary a paper to correct or bulletin board to create. Forfeiting specially arranged classes where future ministers' wives learned to deftly maneuver pieces of silk about their necks, I enrolled in the graduate school instead, earning a master's degree in communications three months before my husband completed his course. I never did master the art of tying a scarf.

In the years and subsequent moves that followed, I have sought to discover richness and meaning in each place that I find myself. Being the wife of a pastor, the concept of life being a horizontal gathering has given me a symbol that makes sense of all the moving and changing that is part of my life. The symbol enables me to glean from my current circumstances that which is unique to that particular setting, without yearning for some ideal environment that will enable me to reach for a vertical prize.

And every situation, I find, has something to offer. I once made a move from a community in which the biggest excitement was stopping the car twice a day for a "cow crossing" to a city in which there were four cars stolen from my block of ten houses in the course of a year. I wouldn't exchange either experience. I've held jobs, by choice, in which I made $4,000 a year, $85 an hour, or nothing at all. I've worked sixty hours a week, twenty hours a week, four hours a week. I've been at the bottom of structures where I've gladly carried out predetermined orders that freed my life from stress and decision making. I've been at the top of structures where I've guided institutions and the layers below me.

And through all of this, I've tried to gather the significance of these experiences, which have become a part of the whole of my life. I've tried to view life not as a one-dimensional progression toward a definable goal but as an empty cup waiting to be filled with the warmth of family relationships, the overflowing richness of friends, the tang of creative endeavor, the fullness of Christian growth.

I guess the surprise for me has been that in the midst of all this living, the tangible rewards have arrived. I certainly never envisioned myself holding a doctoral degree. But there was this child in my family with an enormous amount of energy, struggling to read, trying to find his place in school and life. No one seemed to listen to me when I described his battle. School committees told me I was an overprotective mother. Maybe so, but this overprotective mother wanted answers.

My quest for understanding led me to quit my job as the administrator of a school, negotiate my way by train and subway system into a city I'd never entered, flow with crowds, hail random artists and hurried businessmen for directions, and arrive on the campus of Boston University in the office of the head of the department of special education. "What is it that you'd like to become?" he asked me, as I talked of entering the doctoral program. "That's not the point," I said. "It's what I want to know."

By faith I moved forward, not knowing how this knowledge venture would be financed. I applied for scholarships. Waited.

Applied for others. Held my breath and arrived in the fall with no money to enroll in school and no job to absorb my frustration. I put my children on the school bus. I watched as they were carried away. I realized that in thirty-five years, this would be the first fall I would not be entering an institution of learning. Two days later I received the phone call. The curriculum and teaching department at Boston University needed a graduate assistant. In exchange for teaching two courses, I would be given free tuition.

And so I entered the doctoral program, one semester at a time. Every four months my position ended. Every four months, one or two days before a new semester was to begin, another position was offered to me. Until one cold, gray January. I had exhausted all known possibilities. "No," the department chairs told me. "We won't be needing anyone this semester. You might check downstairs." I went home. I prayed. I cleaned my house.

Gathering the mail from the box, I noticed a small, yellow slip. Certified mail. For some reason, I had an odd premonition that it was from some disgruntled person, a reader of one of my magazine articles, a long-lost student or church member bent on informing me of the error of my ways. The postmaster pushed the envelope through the window. The hollowness in the pit of my stomach increased as I realized that I did not recognize the return address. And then I opened the envelope.

"Dear Mrs. Doran: I was impressed to contact you." Becoming absorbed in the letter, I read of a reader's interest in an article I had written about difficult children. I found a kindred spirit in the mother who told the story of her own son's struggles and her efforts to put his feet on a path to success. Then came the last paragraph. "It is my pleasure and privilege to enclose a memorial gift made out in your name to Boston University in the amount of $1,000 in Thomas' memory. May you and yours be blessed with a happy and prosperous New Year."

Hands shaking, eyes blinded with tears, I drove home.

Sometimes I feel as if I don't deserve the blessings He has showered upon me.

Career woman? No. Just an ordinary child of God trying to find my way on this planet, gathering what I can, searching for meaning, color, and richness along the way. In the pages that follow, I invite you to come along for the journey.

Gathering

INSIGHT

Dale Slongwhite

I have come late to the concept of living life
as a horizontal gathering.
For many years it seemed to me life was a vertical climb
I had somehow failed to make.
"What do you do?" People asked to establish my worthiness.
"Mother," I said for years, then, "Secretary."
Neither seemed to match the achievements of the questioner
nor of myself.

Then Sandra started talking to me about her philosophy
of a horizontal gathering.
I reread copies of letters I had sent.
I meditated on my life.
I gathered the memories of people I have met,
places I have gone, experiences I have weathered or relished.
And I realized I have gathered much.

In this first essay, I will tell you about my life.
In the essays that follow, I will share the things I have gathered
in spite of, or because of,
the things that have or have not happened,

in spite of, or because of,
the fact the mere business of living
has taken so much time, energy, and focus.

I share it with an open hand,
expecting neither agreement nor disapproval,
expecting only that the process of the sharing
will cause you to also reflect on what you have gathered.
Because all of it, everything we have gathered,
is woven into the fabric of the people we have become,
and our stories have value and worth to be shared.

"If you could do it over again," Karen asks me when she is seventeen, "would you marry Dad?"

I stare at her, mind racing, yet devoid of answer. I am caught in a no-win situation. She knows that we married young. She knows that our personalities are dramatically different—we are like a baked Alaska ice-cream sundae. If I say No, will she believe our marriage is a sham? Will she think I regret the last twenty years of my life? If I say Yes, I fear it will give her permission to marry Rick—a young man two years her senior who is doing fair-to-middling academically, has no educational plans beyond his upcoming high school graduation, is loud and controlling, and who assumes she will become his teenage bride.

But I have pledged that my parenting will be honest. She has asked me a question, and I must answer truthfully without intentionally choosing words to manipulate her choices. "It's a good question," I say. "I haven't really considered it before. Would you mind if I thought about it for a week and we could talk then?"

She agrees, and I embark on an examination of the choices that have brought me to this point. Would I arrive here if I had known where I was going? And more specifically, would I have taken the journey with David?

David and I met on July 28, 1967, when we were summer camp counselors at Camp Winnekeag, in Ashburnham, Massachusetts. We were sixteen years old, zealous in our love for the Lord, two kids believing life would reward us for our goodness. He played an amazing game of softball, teaming in the outfield with his fifteen-year-old brother, calling into play his ability to run a five-minute mile. I earned the privilege of taking out the sailfins and decided to impress him by inviting him on a sail of the mile-long lake. We capsized, and I had to admit to him that at 5 feet 1 inch tall, 105 pounds soaking wet or not, although I knew how to right the boat, I lacked the ability to do so. Following my instructions, he accomplished the task. It was a pattern we were to repeat many times over the next twenty years.

At the end of the summer, I entered my junior year at a boarding academy forty miles from his house. David and his brother rose at dawn on registration day and bicycled to the school. They were standing in front of the dorm when I drove up with my parents, and I knew in that moment that he liked me.

He thought I was his exclusive girlfriend, and I was—until March. On my seventeenth birthday, the school held a reverse courtesy formal banquet, and I asked a classmate. For three months I juggled the two boyfriends, leaving one at the front door to exit the back door with the other. My friends watched in awe, wondering how I would manage graduation weekend when both beaus would be in the same place at the same time. Suffice it to say, I didn't manage it well at all and began summer vacation with *no* boyfriend.

Before summer's end we made up, and David transferred to the same boarding academy to stake his claim on my life. At the start of his senior year, age seventeen, he left home never to return, responsible from then on for his soap, deodorant, food, and school bill.

As our senior year wound down, I opened up the college catalog where David intended to go. My father believed that marriage signified adulthood, and that adults should support themselves. I understand this—he had left school before high school graduation to take his place on submarines during World War II and had been self-sufficient ever since. So I knew that if I married, his financial support would end.

Did I want to wait four years to be married? Maybe two ... I turned to the two-year degrees. Nursing—didn't like blood or dealing with other bodily fluids. Bible worker—didn't want to compete in my brother's field. Secretarial—secretarial? I could handle that. And it was in that haphazard manner I determined the course of my life.

Four weeks after earning an associate degree in secretarial science at the age of twenty, I became Mrs. David Slongwhite. I took a job as a clerk in an insurance agency to pay the rent and put food on the table while David finished the last two years of his bachelor's degree. And in a time before computers, I typed dozens of his résumés, sealed envelopes, and stuck on stamps. The early seventies was not a ripe time for aspiring history teachers, and at the last moment, when all other prospects had dried up, David accepted a job in rural Tennessee teaching in a multi-grade classroom in a Christian elementary school.

I had never lived outside of New England nor away from family, but I willingly packed up our few belongings and headed south—excited to be part of Christian education, excited that David was the first person in his family to complete a college education, excited that I would soon be a mother. I believed that all of these things would open up a rosy path before us. As it turned out, our Tennessee days were a time of difficult adjustments.

I corrected student papers, put up bulletin boards, and supported him as a good wife should. I took one college class in the hopes someday I might finish. I sacrificed to the bone when I discovered my husband's employer required him to attend summer school but only paid him ten months out of the year. After fourteen hours of labor, I gave birth to my daughter by Cesarean section and nearly hemorrhaged to death due to incompetent medical care. Before her first birthday, our daughter began having seizures; the pediatrician dismissed them as my imagination.

After two years in Tennessee, I offered a secret prayer letting the Lord know that I was willing to live where He wanted me to live, but if He wanted to know what I really wanted, I'd like to be in Middletown, Connecticut. Several months later, David was invited to teach in that very city in another Christian elementary school.

The first thing I did upon arriving on familiar turf was to make two doctor appointments—one to discuss Karen's seizures with a pediatric neurologist and one for me because I was five months pregnant. Both were wise choices. Within days, Karen's seizures intensified, and I was sent to bed because I was dilated to five centimeters. I stayed there for two months while David unpacked our belongings, prepared meals, and wallpapered around me. Then came the fall.

On the first day of school, I watched David hesitantly walk out the door with a bagged lunch, his face etched with concern. "Will you be OK?" he asked, wavering between his responsibility to the church's children and his own.

"Of course," I said, trembling inside. That night I was hospitalized, and three days later Laurel was born eight weeks prematurely. She remained hospitalized for two weeks after birth. I went home to care for nineteen-month-old Karen, who, one evening, had multiple seizures over a two-hour period. I carried her down one long corridor after another at a different hospital fifteen miles away from her sister, not sure if I should be doing this one week after giving birth.

When Laurel was eighteen months and Karen was three years,

I took a few evening classes at a college to stimulate my brain beyond Captain Kangaroo. Philosophy. Sociology. Marketing. Classes where adults would talk on adult topics. Six months later, at the invitation of a personnel director I met in one of the classes, I took a job working four evenings a week typing and filing and answering phones. The sixty daytime personnel had gone home. Besides my own clacking of typewriter keys, the only sound was the hum of machines on the other side of the wall—the second shift manufacturing skis.

I held that job for eight years and believed I loved it. Now I realize my love was not for the contracts to be typed, the personnel records to be filed, the blinking light on the phone to be attended to. Rather, I loved it for the flexibility it afforded me to raise my children, the flexibility to support my husband in his endeavors, and the flexibility to care for my home.

When the girls were halfway through elementary school, we moved to an urban area we thought would provide them with a better education, and I was thrust unwillingly into the full-time work force. I battled depression and resentment over the fact that the procurement of money had taken priority over raising my children. I did not know for years—until Karen's college classmates discussed it in Freshman English—that my plight was symbolic of my generation. I was only one of thousands of women caught in the flux of history—behind us stood mothers who held down the home front, ahead of us marched daughters with careers. And many in my generation were torn between two worlds, women forced midstream in their motherhood careers to battle an economy we did not understand.

Slowly I began to realize that a great deal of life concerns itself with survival, and survival in modern society means work for most of us. And I had chosen my lifework on the basis of wanting to get married. I typed thousands of pages, worded and reworded for a superior to sign and take credit for, before I realized that work could be more than something to supplement a husband's income or adjust to a child's schedule. Work could be a reflection of self, and mine was not.

And now Karen has asked if I would do it over again. I try to separate the events of my life from the man I have experienced them with. I think of him learning to gently pack my pilinidol cyst during three months of postsurgical care. I think of him walking the floor in the middle of the night with colicky babies. I think of him sneaking into my office an hour before work on Valentine's Day to put a rose on my desk. I think of him vibrating my legs every night to relieve restless leg syndrome. I think of his sincere prayers. I think of his easy laughter. I think of an album full of pictures—always the same multipocketed bird vest, always the same binoculars to his eyes, only the background changing. And I know what I will answer.

"Maybe," I say to Karen. "And maybe not. What I would do if I could do it over again is pursue my own dreams. Finish my education. Become who my talents would have allowed me to become. And if in that process, the relationship had survived, I would have married him. But if in the process of becoming *me* I had to lose *him*, I guess that's what would have happened."

Seven years have passed since Karen unwittingly called me into an assessment of my life choices. Seven years when I concentrated on developing my dormant self. Years in which I finished a B.A. in communications, attended writing seminars and conferences, interviewed numerous authors, and dug into my soul and did some rearranging. Years in which Sandra shared her concept of life as a horizontal gathering and I reflected on what I have gathered.

Karen went on to marry a hard-working young man she met during her freshman year in a Christian college and to experience many things she had not considered trying when she was single. She appreciates the present moment yet plans for the future by continuing her education at Harvard University's Extension School, graduation within reach. Piece upon piece, choice upon choice, she is involved in the lifelong process of gathering.

If Karen were to ask me the same question today about marrying David, I would answer, "Yes, I would." She has grown past the pivotal times of determining her life's destiny, and I have grown too. In developing my own talents and reconnecting with my inner soul, I have discovered I am in no danger of losing him as I find myself. Of all the things I have gathered, this is the most meaningful of all.

Essay done, I save and exit. My back is stiff from a morning of writing. The tangy aroma of spaghetti sauce David has prepared for lunch beckons me. Soon he will ring the dinner bell, and I will gladly join him.

Gathering

STRENGTH

Sandra Doran

It was my husband who found me in a crumpled mass on the floor beside my computer chair. "Do you want to save?" the prompt on the screen had innocently asked. "Yes," I had indicated, after four months of intensive labor, sixty-two pages of text, and one dissertation proposal complete within a fraction of a deadline. The momentum had been gradually building over the semester, consuming all mental and psychological energy for the final push that Friday afternoon.

"Do you want to save?" Having deprived self and family of all the creature comforts generally taken for granted for the past three months, staring at my computer screen, hands shaking, mind clouding, scorched and famished, jaundiced and glassy-eyed, spent and wasted, I pressed "Yes." And in that single motion saved a blank screen over 87,640 characters that represented my life.

Gently, he picked me up from the floor. Dedicated, he began scanning files, searching the hard drive, pressing keys, exiting and entering screens. A man on a mission, bent on retrieving the vanished verbiage. In the end, he found 84,068 characters.

Weakly, I nodded my thanks. Then, re-seating myself, I sought to re-create the last four pages, knowing that when the click of the front door signaled the return of my oldest son from school, all mental concentration would be gone, the project must be ended. I finished the document at 2:17, just as a pre-adolescent voice trumpeted, "I'm home!"

I don't remember what we ate for supper that evening. I don't remember how I clothed myself or my children the next day. I only remember sitting in church with my two boys, vaguely hearing my husband preach from the front of a semi-full sanctuary, feeling like a blackened shell of a person. There was no casserole waiting in the oven at home. There was not a clean piece of laundry in a drawer. No space devoid of clutter. No groceries stocking the shelves.

In my numbed state, all I could think of was present survival. Could I make it through the church service without crying? Should I get up and seek solace in the ladies' room? If I did, would I be taking the risk of breaking down beyond the point of control? I was fragile, empty, drained of all energy.

Then the thought came to me. *Home.* At forty-one years of age, all I wanted was my mother. My father. *Home.* An hour-and-a-half drive away. Peace. Reassurance. Affirmation. Care.

I spent the rest of the sermon focused on keeping it together. Mentally, I concocted ways of letting my husband know, in as few words as possible, that I would be taking a short trip. My leave-taking must be swift, poised, decisive. If I paused to elaborate on the details, I feared I would break down and lose control in front of a shocked congregation. I had to get out.

Finally, I had my escape route cemented in my mind. I would endure through the sermon, the closing hymn, the final prayer. Then, as soon as the pastors and elders marched out, I would grab my two boys by the hands, exit down the side aisle, briefly communicate my message to my husband at the door, depart through the glass doors, locate my car, point it toward the Interstate, set the cruise control on sixty-five miles per hour, and head south.

As I detected the finale of the sermon, I gathered up my children's collection of papers and pencils, books and jackets, sweaters and Bibles. I located my keys in my purse. I whispered huskily to the two boys, "Get ready to follow me. We're going to Grandma's." Wide-eyed they looked up.

"GRANDMA'S?"

"*SHHH!*" I gestured menacingly. "Just get ready to follow me."

Then it was that I realized my husband had finished his sermon and was making an announcement from the front. "I will be doing something a bit different today. Instead of marching out with the elders, I will be remaining at the front of the church. All those who would like to join in a season of prayer for the upcoming meetings, please come and join me at the conclusion of the service."

Heart stopping, I clenched my keys tighter in my sweaty fist. My game plan. Shattered. Could I walk toward the front of that sanctuary? Could I pass Mrs. Jones, who saw me as a composed, rational pastor's wife? Could I negotiate my way past Sonya Adams, who eagerly gathered the pearls I presented to the teens each week in youth class?

Gathering my resolve, my progeny, and my wits, I swallowed and waited for the usher to stand beside my row. I stood up. I swept Eric, Jr. and Jeff into the aisle. Striding toward the front, one thought reverberated in my mind. *Get out. Get out. Get out. Get out.*

I arrived at Eric's side to find him surrounded by saints all speaking in hushed tones. How could I carry off my plan? Get his attention? Explain the pressure, the energy drain, the numbness? Reaching through the mass, I tapped his shoulder. "I'm out of here," I said simply.

On Interstate 95, the boys fought in the back seat for ninety minutes. I made no attempt to intervene, the spat spiraling in epithets and jabs that jarred my nerves and strengthened my resolve to get out. Get home. Collapse.

Sixty miles later, the exit presented itself. I turned off the highway. Turned down Route One. Turned into the road beside the river. Pulled up to the yellow brick ranch. The driveway and garage were glaringly empty. Fumbling in my key ring, I located a means of entrance. The hum of the refrigerator was all that greeted me as I swept open the kitchen door. Peering into the refrigerator, I took some small comfort from two plastic dishes, labeled with my mother's fine script. "Lasagna." "Scalloped corn."

I microwaved them. I ate a home-cooked meal. It tasted good.

Fumbling in my mother's closet, I found a pair of stretch pants and a Florida sweatshirt, two sizes larger than similar items jammed onto the top shelf of my own closet at home. I put them on. I walked back out to the kitchen. I waited.

After twenty minutes, I penciled a note. "I was here. Drove to Holly's."

Back in the car, I paced myself once again. My sister. Family. Solace. Fifteen minutes away.

She recognized the strain on my face immediately. Piling the couch with afghans, she motioned for me to lie down and uttered the words I will never forget. "I'll take the children." Where she went on that cold December night with her own three children and my two in tow, I'll never know. The door opened, the wind howled, and they were gone.

I felt peace on that couch. Rest came to my exhausted spirit. I slept the undisturbed sleep of one who has never known a doctoral committee.

I awoke to a gentle voice. Someone rubbing my feet. "Are you OK?"

It was my mother. Her voice concerned. Her eyes knowing. "Are you OK?"

And in that moment, I realized that I was.

Gathering

MOMENTS

Dale Slongwhite

I can still see him standing in the backlight of the sliding glass doors, newspaper in hand, twenty-four hours of stubble on his cheeks and chin, silvery hair askew, hearing-aid cord winding its way from his ear to the pocket of his ribbed sleeveless undershirt. His lips were rubbery, unsupported by teeth, and his once-muscley upper arms now fleshy and wrinkled. I was not used to seeing the house in the quiet morning light nor him so vulnerable.

Concern colored his eyes and voice as I entered the kitchen from the back door. "Are you all right?" It was he who asked the question of me . . . *me*—young, healthy, pregnant with my first child, life a canvas with only the backdrop painted.

"Yes," I said, "I'm fine. There was no work today so I asked to leave. This day is for you, Gramps. Whatever you want to do, we'll do. Wherever you want to go, we'll go."

His face lighted up. "Let me get ready," he said. "It won't take long." And he hurried away in the hurry of an old man.

We were three generations living in my parents' Connecticut home that summer. With two months between David's college graduation and his first job as an elementary school teacher in Tennessee, we had moved in and secured temporary work assignments. Due to declining health, Gramps had been forced a few months earlier to relinquish his home of thirty years and take up residence in two finished rooms in the basement.

My job for that particular week was at a nuclear power plant overlooking Long Island Sound. For two days I waited for a burst of inspiration to descend upon a director so I could type a procedures manual he was to write. His inspiration never came. So first thing on day three, I asked, "Will there be any typing today?" I had more important things to do than wait for time to pass. I had a grandfather, no longer able to drive, sitting home alone in the yellow brick house beside the river.

I only had to wait a few moments. "I haven't had breakfast," he said. "Can we go to Dunkin' Donuts?" Now *this* was my grandfather ... awash with smiles, clean shaven, full head of silvery hair slicked straight back partless from his forehead, firm mouth, memorable steel-blue eyes, smart-looking in a solid blue golf shirt with three buttons, places to go, people to see.

"Whatever you want, Gramps," I said. "Whatever you want."

No random donut shop, this. It had to be *Dunkin' Donuts*. It had to be *the* Dunkin' Donuts ... the one five miles south of the house where he used to stop every day on his way to work where my father's machine shop used to be. In 1958, my father rented a machine in a room in a corner of a factory and started a machine-shop business. In the morning, he drove around looking for work. In the afternoon, he set the specifications on his screw machine to manufacture nuts, bolts, and turnbuckles. The next morning, he delivered the parts and looked for more work. As the fledgling business grew, Gramps, then retired, took over the deliveries. He loved driving all over southeastern Connecticut in his sea-green push-button Dodge Dart ... after starting his day with a donut.

We sat side by side on stools in front of the counter, our lips white with powder, purple with jelly. He smelled the familiar smells. He felt the familiar feel. He saw the familiar sights. The sugar. The coffee. The padded cushion. The smooth counter. The glass case. The orange booths lined up in front of the plate-glass window.

"What next?" I asked.

"Do you have more time?" he asked, eyes eager, lips a hesitant smile.

"I have all day, Gramps," I said. "This day is for you."

A haircut was next . . . at the old barber in Greenville, at least twenty miles on the other side of the house. "This way," he said, leaning close and pointing a curved, well-tanned finger into the windshield. "A left . . . there . . . that sharp left up that hill." I was not familiar with this section of town where he brought his family to live when my mother was in the eighth grade.

Gramps was born in 1894 in the small country village of Ashton-Under-Lyne, England, one of nine children. When he was a young boy, his father decided to emigrate to the United States. The move took place in two shifts—one year my great-grandfather and his sons came to America to work in the textile factories. They saved enough money to bring my great-grandmother and the girls over the next year. Although my grandfather was only six, he came with the men and was cared for by the owner of the boarding-house where they lived. Before he was nine, he dropped out of school to work beside the men in the textile factories, where he was to remain for more than fifty years.

We passed the mills that day . . . long, long, probably a city block long, red brick, four stories high, broken windows, long abandoned. He pointed out the house on Sixth Street where they lived. The store my Aunt Lucy used to own. The specific parking place to choose in front of the barber shop.

He sat tall in the barber's chair, draped with a white cloth striped in blue. The barber stood behind him with the electric razor buzzing, and they spoke to each other in the mirror. "Not too short," Gramps said.

Fed and preened, he was now ready to visit the machine

shop in its new location. He hadn't been there in several years. David at the drill press, Mom in the office, Dad with blackened oily hands inspecting a small steel part all looked up in surprise when we walked through the door. "What's going on?" they asked me. They couldn't ask Gramps . . . he had only made it two steps through the door. Beaming, he was sharing a story with Lenny, a long-time employee on the turret lathe.

"Just sharing some time," I said. "Some moments and some time."

For most of my growing up years, my mother did not drive. She was chauffeured by my grandfather to the store for groceries, Christmas gifts, the children's back-to-school clothes. Patiently, he sat on benches or windowsills by the checkouts, secretly memorizing the purchases of other shoppers so he could tell us later.

One day my father bought a white Mazda with red interior and parked it in the driveway for Mom. "All of your life," he said to her, "your dad has driven you where you needed to go. The tide is turning, Gloria. You need to be prepared." Sooner than expected, she was the one behind the wheel driving my grandfather to doctor appointments, on errands, to pick out Christmas presents for the family. And that day, it was me.

For lunch, we ate in the car in the parking lot of his favorite takeout. In contented silence we munched on fries and watched other diners back cautiously into parking spots, squeak open doors, fling pocketbooks over shoulders, unstrap babies from car seats, and stride with determined steps toward the entrance. Worn-out, he asked to go home, so we did.

Gramps died three years later, and by that time, I was glad . . . glad that the pain and confusion of disease had finally released its reluctant captive . . . glad that he no longer would have to look death in the face and be afraid . . . glad that the unconquerable foe had finally been conquered.

It took years before I could look through the jagged memory edges of his last debilitating months and see him as he once was. But now I remember . . . I remember him sitting in front of the television set with Joe, the church custodian, watching the Ed Sullivan Show, Lassie, Mr. Ed, laughing way out loud and eating nonpareils and chocolate stars. I remember him learning to play golf at the age of sixty-five, mainly to spend hours on the fairway with his namesake, my brother Mark. I remember the aquarium in his living room, his passion for little-league baseball, his love of fishing. I remember his comment about the dog next door—"I couldn't sleep last night because Boots barked to beat the band!" I remember his unique way of pronouncing words—"*Folly* the man in the *yelly* raincoat who's carrying the *strawbries.*"

And I remember him standing in the backlight of the sliding glass doors, sitting on a stool in a donut shop, chatting with long-time friends beside noisy machines on a long-ago summer day when together we shared a few moments that would never pass our way again.

Gathering

MERCY

Sandra Doran

I don't know why I took up sewing in my teen years. I hated following a pattern, staying within the guidelines when stitching a seam, prodding a machine whose needle sunk into layers of cloth and refused to budge, buzzing at me like an incessant cicada, weaving a tangled web of knotted thread. I suppose it was the selection of the cloth that wooed me back every time, the opportunity to finger tartan plaids, bright cottons, silk, seersucker, dotted swiss. And so I'd optimistically make my selection, leaving the store with yards of fresh fabric and visions of a garment with straight seams, a collar that would lie flat, sleeves that extended to my wrists.

It didn't take long before the vision faded. I had no patience for momentary snags, wheels that wouldn't spin, needles that announced sudden setbacks in thudded pauses. I pressed harder on the pedal, releasing the stubborn machine into jerked compliance, zipping down the side of a dress like a driver at the Waterford Speed Bowl five miles down the road. Once, when plaids didn't match up right on a pair of elastic-waist pants, I decided to wear them backwards. "After all," I reasoned, "the mismatched seams will be less noticeable if I can't see them."

Always in the background was my mother. "Perhaps if you

try it this way ..." "Maybe if you iron the fabric so that it doesn't fold upward while you are trying to sew ..."

Patiently, she sought to guide me, sought to teach me about facing setbacks, disentangling knots, staying within guidelines, keeping a steady pace, persevering when I wished to assign a half-completed garment to the role of dustrag.

One afternoon stands out with clarity, one afternoon when even the iron would not comply, melting the fabric in gluey patches to its steaming underside, marring my attempts at dressmaking with heated finality. I still feel a deep, tearing ache when the memories of that day come swimming to the surface, carrying me back to the intense emotions of adolescence, haphazard thinking, rash action.

I had been pressing the side panel of a bolero vest when it happened, turning the iron higher and higher, trying to force a stubborn seam into submission. The black fabric became shiny at first, sending an acrid odor into the air in warning. Undaunted, I pursued the task, gripping the handle of the Sunbeam appliance in determination, prodding the seam with the pointed end of the instrument. Then it was that I discovered that the fibers of the fabric had broken down, become liquid, adhered to the back of the iron.

In desperation, I brought my plight to my mother, seated in the living room engrossed in her latest find from the public library. "There is another iron in the hall closet," she said, looking up from her book. "Bring me the iron, and I will help you."

To this day I don't know why I interpreted "Bring me the iron" to mean the too-hot instrument in the other room, sizzling and sputtering in silver heat. Thinking only of my ruined vest, the side panel of a bolero marked by a melted vee, I entered the dining room, unplugged the steaming iron, and reappeared before my mother, the overheated instrument in my hand, its cord trailing behind me.

And when I offered it to her, expecting her to grasp the handle, she reached her hands toward the burning metal—those two hands that had grasped mine and led me in my first faltering steps, those hands that had fixed hundreds of my meals, smoothed my sick brow, dried my tears—and I could do nothing but stand there and realize it was too late.

Her flesh bubbled instantly at the touch, reddening, then rising into translucent bubbles across the palms. Her face contorted in agony, those large blue eyes filling with tears, and I thought that I would never deserve the right to live again.

But then, beyond the depths of the torment in her eyes, I read something else—another emotion, a message struggling to take shape.

"I know you didn't mean it," she said, finally. "I'll be OK."

In the midst of physical pain, my mother was actually experiencing another hurt, a deeper, selfless feeling. Beyond the throbbing of flesh, the cruel biting of oxygen on scorched skin, the marring of palms, my mother thought not of her own agony but mine. She was concerned about *me*—Sandra, the one who had offered her the instrument of torture, the foolish, impetuous adolescent who had done such an irrational thing, caused such needless pain.

I managed to return the tiniest flicker of a smile through the tears. And when I remember, three decades later, the deep-tearing agony, there is something else there too. Something that will indelibly be woven into my concept of a *parent*, something that will perpetually guide me in shaping the lives of two young boys, something that will forever make me both anguished and grateful whenever I hear the words, "Father, forgive them, for they know not what they do."

Gathering

T R U T H

Dale Slongwhite

In my childhood home of Protestant father and Catholic mother, God was the originator of all good things. We revered Him as the Almighty who created us. We trusted Him as the all-loving One who held us in the palm of His hand. We bowed our heads in reverence and thanksgiving at mealtimes for what He supplied us. At bedtime, we knelt and asked for the protection we knew He would provide. And each weekend we gathered with others of like faith to praise and worship Him—some on Saturday, some on Sunday. We respected each other without con-frontation because our God was bigger than theological doctrine. Our religion was more encompassing than proving a biblical point. Our God was good and so were we, His creations, because we were made in His image.

From this base, I grew into Christian adulthood, respecting varied forms of worship as emanating from the honest hearts of people who desired to honor their God. I believed that truth was a continuous process of discovery with ever-expanding perim-eters, that life was a gift from God—a gift that I honored by seek-ing happiness and cultivating talents He had hidden within me. I trusted that He always wanted the best for me; therefore, I asked for His guidance and protection. And on those occasions when the best did not happen, I believed the evil force in the universe had sabotaged God's plans and that God mourned along with me; therefore, I sought His comfort.

I believed that He had blessed me with a discerning mind, and I decided to use and develop it to its capacity, to be the best that I could be. I believed that who I was in my heart was more important than what I said or the doctrines to which I claimed to espouse. I believed that my destiny in this world and the next was based largely on the choices I made—God was willing to have me in heaven, did I want to go? If no, behave any way I desired. If yes, incorporate His principles into every aspect of my daily life.

I took Micah 6:8 as a dictum, "He hath shewed thee, O man, what is good; and what doth the Lord require of thee, but to do justly, and to love mercy, and to walk humbly with thy God."

It was years before I realized my viewpoints were controversial. I was well into my thirties before I figured out that argumentative, scripture-dissecting, narrow definers of truth were not just an occasional voice crying from the wilderness. They were a force—a large, loud, convincing force to be reckoned with.

So I listened. If that was God's expectation of me, I needed to know.

I listened to countless sermons defining me as wretched, decrepit, and grossly sinful—sermons that admonished me to rise from my state of doom and be satisfied with nothing less than perfection. I sat through dissertations on the ugliness of the world, with heaven at the end as the only reason to endure the daily life. I witnessed shouting matches regarding the punctuation or rightful translations of minute Greek words in the Bible. I listened to a weeping young woman share that all she had ever wanted out of life was to be a mother. Upon discovering she was infertile, she believed God had purposely taken from her the one thing she desired in order to test her as He had Eve with the tree in the

Garden of Eden. She vowed to trust Him, to prove to Him that she was worthy, and that she loved Him no matter what He did to her.

And as I listened, I had a hard time worshiping a God who had created a world with all the good things gone. I found it difficult to set aside my desire to make good choices and view myself as a despicable being who could do no good, as one who must seek perfection when all I ever wanted was excellence. I found it masochistic to crawl to God seeking comfort if I believed Him to be the one who had caused the pain. I judged it petty to be more concerned with jots and tittles than honesty and intentions.

I liked the God of my youth. It is to Him I have returned in midlife ... a God who created the cultural differences of Chinese, Mayan, Egyptian, and Eskimo; therefore, I will respect. A God who splashed the universe into infinity; therefore, I will not restrict. A God who sent us Jesus as a mentor; therefore, I will love, not judge. A God who looketh on the heart; therefore, I will concentrate on mine. A God whose love I will not confuse with the powers of darkness.

I realized that the search for truth is an unending process and that it is important to understand the base upon which we choose to build it. For in the same way we perceive God, we will perceive and value ourselves, others, and the whole business of conducting our daily lives as well.

Gathering

RICHNESS

Sandra Doran

When I was in the first grade, the teacher casually mentioned that everyone, in the course of a lifetime, would consume at least one tablespoonful of dirt. My eyes opened wide in disbelief.

"*Everybody?*" I queried.

"Everybody," she assured me.

That established, I decided to face the inevitable. That afternoon, tablespoon in hand, I headed for the small patch of earth beside our two-toned gray house on Perkins Avenue. It didn't take much to dig into the blackness and fill the spoon with a hard, dark clod that extended over the edges. But consuming it was another matter.

"*Everybody* has to do it," I reasoned in the gray gloom of that early November day. "It's better to get it over with now. Then I won't have to worry about it for the rest of my life." Determined, I counted to ten, opened mouth, inserted spoon, worked upper and lower jaws, choked, and washed it down with the hose.

Following my childhood reasoning, I've had thirty-seven dirt-free years since that afternoon. But I suspect that if truth be told, this female human will have consumed two tablespoonfuls of dirt by the end of her lifetime.

From my earliest days, my actions always seem to have been

governed by what some would term *deferred gratification pattern.* Work now. Play later. Memorize your times tables before jumping into the pool. Pay the bills before indulging in a living-room suite. Take an academic course before learning to paint. Consume the cold, gritty reality of life's hard clods early; tomorrow you will be grateful.

A study was conducted in which young children were given a marshmallow and then told that if they hadn't consumed it by the time the teacher came back, they would receive three more. Had I been in the study, I wouldn't have even eaten the three more, hoping that my conscientiousness would result in an increased reward later on.

Deferred gratification pattern can lead to some great things: advanced degrees, extra marshmallows, clean attics. But I've found that if I don't make a conscious effort to seize the richness that God has placed in each day, I stand to miss the blessings of the here and now. And as I scan my memory banks for moments of meaning, it is not the deferring I recall but the living.

I remember a rare evening in Cortland, New York, more than a decade ago, when a friend showed up at my doorstep of an evening, totally unencumbered, her three children being cared for by their father. On an impulse we rushed out to the garage, pulled the bikes down from their hooks, strapped my one-and-a-half-year-old into the infant seat on the back of mine, and pedaled off into the coolness of the night. Up one avenue and down the next we maneuvered the ten-speeds, like two delinquents, our hair blowing back with the breeze, our hearts beating with the exertion.

We arrived in the center of the small country town twenty minutes later and parked our bikes before a cafe boasting such chalkboard specials as broccoli soup, vegetable lasagna, and homemade whole-wheat bread. Inside, we treated ourselves like royalty. My baby reached out from his highchair, periodically grabbing at the small, round table and threatening to send our dinner to our laps. But even that didn't mar the moment. We were two women, out of sync with the normal routine of our days, sharing a meal and a country evening.

In Bridgeport, Connecticut, amid city streets unsuitable for even daytime bicycle excursions, an equally memorable day stands out. The January afternoon seemed, at first, to hold little promise. Outside, the sky threatened to suffocate all light with its gray and heavy wraps. Inside, my husband and son sought to sleep off the misery of parched throats, draining sinuses, and throbbing heads.

And then a single ray of light found an opening in the clouds. Others followed, brightening the out-of-doors alive with a spring like quality. Picking up the telephone, I rang up Primrose, a graduate student from Zimbabwe whose friendship I had come to treasure. Within an hour, we were weaving in and out of city traffic, map spread out in the front seat, seeking to discover a spot we had circled in red.

After entering and exiting the same major highway at least three times, we turned to the left, down an unlikely street, and, just about ready to turn around in despair, discovered a sign. Two more miles, and we had arrived.

Flinging open the car doors, we drank in deeply of salt air and unexpected sunshine. Before us the Atlantic Ocean sparkled, set off by an abundance of texture-weathered, splintered docks; coils of heavy rope; an overturned masthead; a huge, rusty anchor; bits of ice clinging to railings and boardwalk; holiday wreaths gracing the fronts of streamlined white cabin cruisers. Unzipping my camera bag, I took off at a trot like the proverbial kid in a candy store. Another day to live, another blessing for which to give thanks.

In Saratoga Springs, New York, a day in early spring joins the vivid bank of images forming a permanent part of my conscious memory. Looking back into the Adirondack Mountains, I see an impatient stream rushing down a wooded hill; three pairs of feet exploring its depths; four sneakers and two scuffed moccasins on a rocky bank.

And further back in the files of my memory still, an early fall day is etched so vividly that even the passing of the years cannot mute its colors. The college semester had barely begun, but already we struggled with papers, lists of anatomical appellations, conjugated verbs, and dates of historical significance. Yet on that Sunday, with the sun blazing with the borrowed brightness of a summer's day, we could not sacrifice ourselves to the cool hum of the water fountain and the pale fluorescence of the library.

Out into the fields we wandered, Ida and I, devoid of coats and books, Ted grasping a watercolor pad, colors, and brushes. He painted us up on the hill, sprawled on the ground, leaning on elbows, facing the view before us with all the promise of two freshmen on a golden fall afternoon. I would do anything to hold that painting in my hands today, to experience again the feeling of being an eighteen-year-old student, evading responsibility just for one day.

But the day in South Lancaster has come and gone; likewise the days in Cortland, Saratoga, and Bridgeport. Yet stolen moments still beckon—walks in the snow when dishes pile up in the sink; excursions to Boston, with Eric and Jeff tracing patterns on the windows of the commuter train while my paperwork lies undone at home; romps on beaches with unwritten manuscripts buzzing in my head.

In the final analysis, I have decided that it is not so much the gratification that I must defer but the deferring.

Gathering

COMMON BONDS

Dale Slongwhite

"I don't know how you'd feel about this," Laurel said. "But
I'd like to invite the men home for dinner."

"The men?" I asked, failing at my attempt to mask shock.
"Why?"

"We're trying to get them out more. Interact with regular
people. And they keep asking about you. So I just thought . . . but
if you're not comfortable, I'd understand. Just think about it."

"The men" were three individuals in their midthirties who
were developmentally challenged and hearing impaired. At nineteen, Laurel was enrolled in the second year of a sign-language
interpreter program and had taken the job in the group home to
practice her sign language.

We knew about the men through humorous stories she told.
Once after she had her shoulder-length locks restyled to a crewcut,
one of the men asked if she'd joined the army. "Me and you," he
signed. "Me and you together in the army." Another time, she'd
gone to an amusement park with them and accompanied one
man into the haunted house. Ten feet into the exhibit, she and
her charge were so scared they fought their way out the entrance
door, much to the opposition of the grim reaper who insisted it
was against the rules.

And we knew about the men because we'd seen them briefly. One was curious about Laurel's parents and stood guard at the window of the home near the end of her shift. When we drove up, he bolted out the door and tapped insistently on the window until I could no longer feign oblivion. Cautiously, I rolled down the window part way. He pointed past me at David then back at himself, making exaggerated outlines of his stomach. Laurel arrived at that moment to interpret. "Jack thinks you're a man if you have a belly," she said. "He thinks the two of you qualify." David's short laugh revealed his embarrassment over the intended compliment.

Nevertheless, we did not *know* the men, and I was not eager to alter that status. I rationalized my feelings by questioning what I had in common with grown men who could barely hear or communicate and who were operating on a child's level. But I suspected that deep within, I might uncover something else . . . fear, maybe. Fear of not knowing what to do if something went awry during the visit. Fear of facing what I did not understand. Or maybe even fear of actually discovering we had something in common after all.

"You won't have to do anything," Laurel assured me. "I'll be the one in charge. I'll take care of everything. But I'll bring another staff member just in case . . ."

In the end I agreed—not out of graciousness to the invited guests but rather as a gesture to affirm my teenager's compassion toward those who were handicapped.

We decided on Sunday at 1:00 p.m. The morning of the event, I vacuumed and dusted. I made lasagna in the company pan. I put all the extensions in the dining-room table and ironed the long guest tablecloth. I set stemware beside the best dishes. I baked a cake, tossed a salad, mixed the punch. Throughout the preparations, I kept reassuring myself with the thought, "Just pretend you're having regular company." And every few minutes, I glanced nervously out the window.

When Laurel pulled the twelve-passenger van into the drive-way, I was shocked—she really *was* the one in charge. Despite what she said, I hadn't pictured my youngest child driving a large vehicle fifteen miles down the highway with the lives of four other people in her hands.

Van doors opened. Men uncertainly eased themselves to the ground, their puffy winter jackets zipped to their chins, red knit hats pulled to their eyebrows. Eyes focused on Laurel, they waited for instructions.

"They're here," I called to David and watched the men plod a weaving path to the house. The front door opened, and a man with Down's syndrome stepped over the threshold. As David and I moved forward to greet him, he grabbed the collar of his coat with both hands and emitted a jarring shriek that froze us in our tracks midway across the room.

My mind raced, searching for a proper reaction, and then Laurel squeezed through the doorway around him, smiling. She swooped up our white cat, Leo. "Sorry," she said. "He's afraid of cats. Been talking about it all day. Mom, Dad, I'd like you to meet Dan." She handed me the cat and introduced us in sign. Word-lessly, Dan walked past us into the living room, scanning the room from floor to ceiling.

Next, Laurel introduced Jack, a compact, animated man. He recognized David immediately and made the stomach gestures again, pointing back and forth between them. He shook my hand and spoke in garbled monotones. "Yes," Laurel said pleasantly. "This is my Mom."

Before I could respond, a large man whizzed between us. "That's Cliff," Laurel said. "He doesn't communicate too well, but he'll be fine. Cliff does everything in a hurry. Eats fast. Walks fast. Cleans his room fast."

"Send him over when it snows," I joked. "We'll put him to

work on the driveway!"

Sue, the second staff member, was last through the door. I had just enough time to register that she was a year or two older than Laurel before noticing all three men investigating the master bedroom. "Laurel . . ." But she was already on top of it. Signing and talking, comfortable and smiling, she said, "Yes, this is my parents' room. My room? Sure. Come on . . ." She started up the steps shadowed by three eager men.

They loved the dinner. Cliff finished his first helping before the rest of us were served. I was just beginning to relax when Jack pointed to me and uttered a few unintelligible words. Laurel laughed. "No-o-o-o," she said, shaking her head and signing. "You cannot kiss my mother. You only met her today. You need to know someone longer than one day before you kiss them. Don't worry, Ma. He's pretty good about respecting boundaries."

Half a slice of cake was still on my plate when all three men donned their coats. We'd asked them for dinner, and they'd taken it literally. They'd eaten, so it must be time to go. No lingering for this group. No small talk or sharing in the living room.

Jack passed me on the way to the door. "Goodbye," I said.

He turned to me, eyes alight with excitement. "I heard that!" he said, and this time I understood. "I heard that! Say it again! Say it again!" He edged closer until his ear was half an inch from my mouth.

"Goodbye, Jack," I said again.

Smiling, Jack took a few steps forward then stopped. Ten feet from the door stood Dan, mannequin-like. Between him and his means of exit sat our cat, Leo. I watched Jack stand silent for a few moments, allowing the situation to register. He looked from Dan to the cat to the door, back to the cat, back to Dan. Then he walked heavily forward, awkwardly picked up Leo, brushed past Dan, and wordlessly thrust the cat into my arms. Together the men turned and walked out the door.

When the van passed the window where David and I stood waving, the two women in the front seat smiled and returned the wave. In the back seat, one man held an empty gaze while two stared intently at the house.

For days, Jack and Dan told everyone about their dinner engagement. "Ate at Laurel's house," they signed. "Laurel's mother. Laurel's father." Jack added another line that took Laurel awhile to decode. "4-5," he signed. "4-5." Eventually it dawned on her—it was the number of our house.

For days they talked . . . for years I have talked . . . about the afternoon Jack, Dan, and Cliff came to visit. They were men, I discovered in spite of myself, regular men with whom I had much in common. Curiosity about the lives of people we rub shoulders with. Anticipation of events outside our regular routine. A yearning for companionship. Hunger and favorite ways to satiate it. The search for a common bond. Love and the desire to express it. The need to memorize embellishing details. Fear. Eagerness to alleviate another's fear. Positive response to kindness. Excitement in unexpected communication. Chilled by the cold. Warmed by remembrance.

And from Laurel that day I caught but a glimpse of something she intrinsically possesses—an understanding of the nebulous balance between accepting limitations and respecting the God-given humanness of us all.

Gathering

UP THE PIECES

Sandra Doran

"Telling Your PreSchooler About Death." I glanced at the flier briefly then decided to attend. The mother of two preschool boys, I felt I could use all the help I could get in dealing with the complicated issues life sent my way. And so I sent my two charges downstairs with the children's librarian and settled in to listen to what the experts had to say about a very delicate subject.

Taking notes on a yellow legal pad, I mentally agreed with all that the lecturer advised. Children should not be sheltered from the realities of life. Death should be seen as a natural thing. The obvious conclusion of existence. Part of the natural cycle. All of us will die someday. We cannot avoid the inevitable.

I looked up to see other mothers, too, taking down the particulars, anxious to record the wisdom of the experts. If a pet dies, the speaker continued, a family has an excellent opportunity to discuss death. The truth should not be kept from the child but rather expressed in a candid, matter-of-fact manner. Children should be allowed to grieve. The pet should be buried with some ceremony.

All of it made so much sense. The days of secrecy—about sex and crime and dying—were over. My generation was an enlightened one, free, open, direct. Our children would not be spared and sheltered but equipped, informed, prepared.

And then Mickey died.

It would have been easier if he had died on a day when Eric felt accepted in the neighborhood. But as fate would have it, Mickey chose to expire on a day when a white mouse was the only thing in the world between a little boy and loneliness.

I saw Eric from the window, running toward the house with tears streaming down his face, the other children mocking in the background. "They don't want to be my friends," he lamented. "They said there's a secret club, and I can't be in it."

His voice broke for a minute, and then his face brightened. "Well, I'll just play with Mickey. He's still my friend."

My husband had purchased the small rodent two weeks before, on a morning when I was at work, shocking me with the news when I walked in the door. But my initial reaction had been tempered by the effect Mickey seemed to have on our five-year-old son. Gone were the pleas for someone to stay in his room "just a little bit longer" at bedtime. Gone were the afternoons when "nobody wants to play with me" haunted my every step as I carried out my duties around the house. Mickey filled the void. A pet all his own—not to be touched by baby brother—Mickey became for Eric the friend he so desperately needed.

I beat Eric to the aquarium in his room and stooped to look through the glass at the tiny white mouse. I stared, unbelieving, at the still form, the open eyes. Then I headed Eric off at the door.

"I bought some new cookies today. Let's go have a couple." Temporarily avoiding the issue, I steered him to the kitchen. My husband walked in as we munched our chocolate chips and looked at me, questioning. I gave him a covert look and motioned toward the stairs. Five minutes later he was back down again, his grave look confirming my suspicion.

"I'll be back," he said. "I'm going to the mall."

There was no question as to the purpose of his mission and

no heading Eric off any longer. Finishing his cookies, he ran for the steps. "I want to get Mickey now," he said.

"Why don't we play cars," I tried weakly. But it was too late.

Up in his room, Eric was calling down to me. "Mickey is not in his cage. Where is he, Mom?"

In that split second I made a decision. I had heard the advice of the experts. I knew how to tell a preschooler about death. I was armed with five pages of yellow legal paper on honesty, openness, candor.

"Dad is taking him to the vet's to get a shampoo," I answered.

Eric fairly danced with excitement, rushing outside, hailing neighbors, calling to anyone who would listen, "My mouse is getting a shampoo!" I raised not the hint of an eyebrow at the turned heads, incredulous faces.

Back on our own porch, I heard the phone ringing and ran inside. "They're all out of mice at the mall," came my husband's voice. "I'm heading for the pet store, twenty miles south."

We spent the afternoon at the park, Eric spirited and anxious for the return of his pet, myself willing the hands of my wristwatch to circle the face in haste. After Eric had jumped on the spring-loaded lion more times than he could count, pumped his legs on the swings until he was dizzy, climbed the ladder and descended the slide more times than all the apparatus combined in the game "Chutes and Ladders," he could be held off no longer.

"Let's go, Mom. Mickey should be home by now."

Gripping his hand, I thought of his father, borne on a mission of the heart, sharing a secret that could shatter a young boy's heart. We arrived at home to discover the returned car in the driveway. Inside, I spotted a few clues. The scent of Clorox. A freshly opened box of cedar chips on the kitchen counter.

"I decided to clean out the cage to get it all ready for your mouse," came a voice from upstairs.

Eric could contain himself no longer. "Let me see him!" he

shouted as he rushed for the stairwell. Close behind him, I entered the room and caught my husband's eye for one long moment as he produced a small, square box. Eric thrust his hand out eagerly, grasping the tiny white rodent whose tail, I couldn't help but noting, was just a tad bit shorter than Mickey's.

"Look how CLEAN he is!" he exclaimed. And then, as his faithful little friend escaped from his ardent clutch, "Boy! He's wound up today."

Eric and "Mickey" played for the rest of the afternoon—across paper-toweled streets and around table legs. The sound of the other children playing outside floated through the window every so often, but Eric didn't seem to hear.

Finally it was time for bed, and Eric gently lowered "Mickey" into his glass aquarium home. After the routine of washing up, brushing teeth, and saying his prayers, Eric snuggled beneath his covers.

"Mom?" he said after I had tucked him in, looking up at me in the semidarkness with large, serious eyes. "I love Mickey. I'm never going to let anything happen to him."

Standing over his vulnerable form wrapped in a Sesame Street blanket, I resolved the same for him.

Gathering

KNOWLEDGE

Dale Slongwhite

"If I go back to school," I asked David when I was forty-one, "will you do the laundry?"

"No problem," he said so easily I wondered why I hadn't posed the question years earlier.

Twenty-one years before, I had graduated with an associate's degree in secretarial science, and it had always bothered me that I never completed a four-year degree. It seemed like unfinished business, and I wondered where I would have been or what other opportunities would have presented themselves if I had a bachelor's degree. Karen was a freshman in college, and Laurel was a senior in high school. Their demands on my time were not as great as when they were younger, and if I were to finish college before them, I would have to do it quickly. I was working as an administrative assistant at Atlantic Union College (AUC), and Sandra encouraged me to ask the director of the Adult Degree Program to assess my transcripts.

Three years after graduating with an A.S. degree, I had driven twenty-five miles down narrow, windy roads in east Tennessee to take an evening class in *Introduction to Education* at a community college. It was my first experience driving after dark, and to make it more difficult, I left behind our newborn daughter in

David's care. One evening driving to school, I detected a strange tinkling sound from beneath the hood. I raised the radio volume so I wouldn't have to cope with it and stopped at the nearest garage, twenty miles later. The mechanic had a hard time understanding my Yankee accent, and I had to ask him to repeat every line of his southern drawl. What I thought he said was, "Drive sixty miles per hour on the highway, and you'll be OK."

After class I followed his instructions, only to have the engine throw a rod on a particularly dark and lonely stretch of road. When the first car drove by fifteen minutes later, I abandoned my own vehicle and accepted a ride with a stranger. I finished the class but couldn't get up the nerve to return the next semester. For that experience, AUC would accept three hours of transfer credits. One baby step toward a bachelor's degree.

Two years after I took the class in Tennessee, David accepted a job in Connecticut, and I enrolled in evening classes at another community college to keep my sanity. Karen was two and a half and having seizures. The medication to control the problem caused hyperactivity. On one trying day when I was sweeping the kitchen, I noticed she was throwing things into the toilet. I dropped the broom and ran into the bathroom. She scooted between my legs, picked up the broom, and unswept the pile. When I turned and saw what she was doing, she ran off, grabbed a penny, and tried to stick it in an electrical socket. Laurel, who was nearly a year old, was a baby whose unceasing cries could rarely be comforted.

So I enrolled in a few classes where adults would talk on adult topics. All day I gave my attention to the needs of my daughters. But two evenings a week, I left supper-cleanup and baby-bathing to their father while I learned about the latest selling concepts in a marketing class, defended the existence of God in an ethics class, and studied social problems much greater than my own in a sociology class. AUC would grant me nine hours of transfer credits. Three more baby steps towards a bachelor's.

Then came a long dry spell. David enrolled in a computer-certificate program. I worked part time in the evenings, and later, full time days. School couldn't be wedged into an overloaded schedule.

During this time I decided to write a book. I spent a year writing and editing, a year circulating the manuscript to over a dozen publishers, and I was shocked every time a rejection slip came in the mail. How could it be? I believed myself to be a good writer and had put everything into this book. What didn't I know? Only one way to find out. In the public library, I researched colleges within a one-hour radius of my home, called and asked, "Do you have any classes in writing?"

After a twelve-year absence I returned to the classroom, this time in the first writing class of my life. Over the next two years, I took two more. Those three semesters, I was energized beyond description by the writing assignments. I worked full time, completed my homemaker tasks, made myself available to my daughters, but always in my mind floated strong verbs, succinct paragraphs, my own voice as I shared original works in class. Nine more credits chipped away that AUC would accept in transfer.

One day I looked over my seven college transcripts and decided to get serious. All of these college classes had to amount to something; namely, a degree. A quick review of the area colleges revealed that degrees attainable in the evening were overwhelmingly concentrated in business. I grudgingly left writing classes for U.S. Government and Statistics. *Chip. Chip.*

And then I took the job as administrative assistant to the vice president of Academic Affairs of Atlantic Union College, and Sandra came for a visit. "I've spoken to Ottilie," she said. "She'll look over your transcripts and give you direction on how to pull it all together."

Two years part time, the director of the Adult Degree Program said, and I'd have a bachelor's in communications. With a clear-cut reachable goal, I marched into the Registrar's office and signed up for a literature class, which met during my lunch hour, and a 5:00 p.m. photography class. Twice a week I raced across campus to the English Department, wolfing down a sandwich. Countless evenings I spent in the muted light of the darkroom, thinking of nothing else but the materializing images on the photography paper. The hypnotizing clunk-clunk of the water-bath sink lulled me into a false sense of relaxation, but the 10:00 p.m. winter air snapped me back into reality for the forty-mile ride home.

For three more semesters, I took classes on campus—a noontime class in rituals that dramatically affected my parenting; a PageMaker class that later helped me land a job writing a corporate newsletter; and the most mind-stretching class of my quarter-century college career—a small 5:00 p.m. philosophy class taught by two renowned professors. We sat around a conference table week after week discussing St. Anselm's Ontological Argument, Descarte's theory that reality exists only in the mind, and Kierkegaard's belief that if passion is eliminated, faith no longer exists. We munched on cheese twists and wheat thins to stave off our hunger.

Since I was part of the Adult Degree Program, I also completed personally-designed projects. For a full year I studied four New England writers—read their works, procured interviews in their homes, attended their public readings, photographed them, developed the photographs in the darkroom, and wrote lengthy reaction papers. I journeyed out of state to interview a writer who had just returned from a book-signing tour of India and had recently been featured in a television special. I interviewed a woman whose book had been made into a movie by Steven Spielberg. I spoke to a professor who had beaten five hundred contenders to win the Iowa Short Fiction Award.

I gathered all my courage and drove into the heart of Boston to interview a woman in a cozy basement apartment who turned out to be a kindred spirit. She told me that one day she was lying on the beach at Martha's Vineyard with a friend, dreaming about *becoming* a writer. Suddenly she sat up, looked at her friend, and said, "I'm going to *be* a writer now and stop dreaming about *becoming* a writer in the future!" In relating the experience, she said that to hold onto a dream, you always have it, but if you try and then fail at the one thing you hold dear, what do you have left? On the other hand, the thought of growing old and bitter at never having reached for her dream was too much, and she decided to take the risk.

Twenty-five years after I started the journey to a bachelor's degree, I marched down the aisle to celebrate success. Part of my job at the college was to orchestrate the details of graduation. That year I did so in a robe and mortarboard. I stood at the door to the auditorium directing the processional then stepped into line when the *S*s marched by. "You're on your own!" I called to the rest of the alphabet.

From Massachusetts to Tennessee to Connecticut to New Hampshire and back to Massachusetts I have gathered knowledge. And even as I wonder where I would be today if I had graduated from college twenty-three years earlier, I know that I would not trade what I have gathered for whatever the unknown could have offered.

My conscience would allow me to extend it no farther—a year after graduation I reminded David why he had agreed to take over the laundry, and once again I became the responsible party. But his habit is ingrained. Even now, four years postgraduation, as I sit in my study and write, I can hear the thump of his footsteps on the basement stairs, water rushing into the washing machine, the squeak of our old dryer. And I know that in the top drawer of my dresser are socks I did not put there, neatly folded, neatly stacked.

Gathering

COURAGE

Sandra Doran

In my family growing up, you never said anything that might offend anybody. My father once choked down a second plateful of an indefinable colloidal casserole because he had done such a good job convincing a relative that he liked the first helping. You did what you were asked, reacted graciously to governors and panhandlers alike, trusted, smiled, nodded, and drank extra glasses of water when things were a bit difficult to swallow.

As an adult, I found myself not only vulnerable but unable to turn back after I'd made a decision. Once, when daylight saving time robbed me of an hour, I raced out of my driveway in Berrien Springs, Michigan, late for a meeting. "You're going the wrong way," my husband called after me. "I don't have time to turn around," I yelled back.

A compulsion to be nice. An inability to turn back. A prescription for trouble.

When I was a young pastor's wife, I accompanied my husband to a halfway house where he conducted Bible studies at the request of one of the residents. Each week we were joined by a group of sincere young men struggling to deal with their own emotions, feelings, and psychological conflicts. I noticed, after the first month, that one young man, Raymond, had dropped out of the group. "Where is Raymond?" I asked Roger, who was chewing on his nails in the corner of the couch.

"He can't take this religion stuff." He spat out a nail into an ashtray balanced on the edge of a chair beside him. "He gets real scared when people start talking religion. Real scared."

Poor Raymond, I thought. That night I prayed that Raymond would feel comfortable enough to return to the group the next week.

The following Tuesday evening, Raymond was comfortable enough. He sat on the couch, stared at my husband, uttered not a word while the men discussed their problems and challenges. *But he's here,* I thought, *and that's a start.*

After the study, Raymond approached me. "Mrs. Doran," he asked. "Would you like to see my paintings?"

"I'd love to. You paint, Raymond? How wonderful! I had no idea."

He smiled, his lips curling upward for the first time all evening. "Follow me," he said. "The paintings are in my room up-stairs."

I swallowed. I had expected Raymond to bring the paintings down to the living room. But I had told him I wanted to see them. How could I tell him that I had changed my mind, that no, I really didn't care whether he painted or not. He had not been to the studies in weeks. He was just beginning to show an interest in the Bible. To refuse to follow him would show a lack of trust, be an affront on his personhood. Following Raymond to his room was a risk. But the greater risk would be to assume he meant harm when none was intended. I couldn't consciously offend anybody. There was no way out.

I moved as if in a dream, feeling as if I were going to my fate. Passing my husband in the hall engrossed in a conversation with one of the residents, I tried one last-ditch effort. "Raymond would like to show us some paintings . . ." my words trailed off, unregistered, unheard.

At the top of the stairs, Raymond opened the door to the first room on the right. On a cot against the wall slept another young man, clad only in his underwear. My heart froze. But never, in the midst of the drama, did I think of running for the door, confronting Raymond, escaping to safety. I had started a series of events. There was no way back, no way out.

Raymond pulled a chair from his desk into the center of the room. "Sit down," he instructed.

Handing me an armful of canvasses, he busily pulled up a small footstool, removed my shoes, and seated himself on the floor. I looked through the canvasses quickly, noting the female form portrayed in various angles on the crude sketches. "These are very nice, Raymond," I faltered. "You appear to have a real talent for art." Inwardly, I prayed, "Whatever is happening here, Lord, just get it over with fast."

It wasn't until the next week that one of the residents told us about Raymond's foot fetish. For all I knew, I was being raped, starting from the outer appendages on up. But Raymond's obsession with my toes was quickly brought to an end.

With a bang, the bedroom door suddenly flew open. "Raymond, what are you doing?" my husband demanded. "Sandy, get up."

I backed out of the room, still in role. "Thank you for showing me the pictures, Raymond," I said.

We were almost home before I cried. I lamented the fact that I had worn shoes that showed the cleavage of my toes. I vowed to wear army boots every Tuesday night for the rest of my life. I felt guilty for not being able to turn back, for walking into a trap with my eyes open, for following Raymond up the steps, heart pounding, panicked, seemingly stuck.

But it wasn't until the following week that I vowed to make a permanent change in the over-politeness that caused my vulnerability. "You should have seen my Mama outside of the library last week," said the five-year-old daughter of a shy, pastor's wife friend of mine.

"What happened?" I turned to her two brothers, already laughing by her side.

"Some man in the library looked at her funny," said the older boy. "Then he followed Mama out to the car. She whirled around so fast you wouldn't believe it. Then she said, 'Are you looking at me? Well, you better not be!' We've never seen her so mad!"

Linda? Shy, introverted Linda? The same Linda who appeared afraid to speak out in group discussions while I dominated the conversation? This same Linda confronted a stranger? Took a risk at offending someone who may have meant her no harm?

Something inside me changed then. I started hanging up on telemarketers. Not letting every random person that knocked on my door into my living room. Turning around when I found myself getting lost, late at night, in strange places. Once, when an anonymous caller harassed me for days with his silent presence on the other end of the line, I took great delight in placing a police whistle by the phone, blowing his hammer and anvil into his semicircular canal.

I like to think that I haven't become cold, unfeeling. I still pile large helpings of unidentified, unpopular items on my plate at potlucks to assure anonymous people that their offerings are palatable. I still avoid offending. I still sit and eat with the anxious, ill-shaven gratefuls at our church soup kitchen while others serve. But let one of them get anywhere near my feet under the table, and he may have a difficult time walking home. The army boots come in handy that way.

Gathering

RITUALS

Dale Slongwhite

Karen came home after her freshman year in college speaking to us through gritted teeth, each word deliberately enunciated, punctuated with daggers shot from the eyes. "I don't think I should have to ask *permission* to do anything," she said. "Kathy drove to New Orleans and never asked her parents if she could go. Diane does whatever she wants and doesn't have to ask."

I laughed. "Those parents didn't have control of their daughters when they were eight," I said. "I've never looked to them as role models."

Her jaw tightened. Her back stiffened. She headed for her room. I called to her retreating shadow, "I'll think about it. We'll talk over the weekend."

For the next five days, I did think. I thought of all the troubles teens bring upon themselves and their families because of poor decisions. I thought about the powerful influence they have upon each other. I thought of how badly I wanted to protect her from the masked evils in life.

David and I had lengthy conversations. It seemed to us the launching stage of parenting was the most difficult because there are so few guidelines at this juncture. Our role as parents during other stages was clear. During infancy, it meant sustaining life.

During the young years, it meant teaching social skills and obedience, imparting a love of reading, learning, and nature. During the early and midteen years, it meant candid discussions on sexuality, drugs, goals, responsibility, the value of an education. It meant re-evaluating the concept of right and wrong we had developed in the sixties to honestly see what applied to the nineties. It meant questioning what to hang onto, what to let go of.

But the launching stage—the time to say "I have done what I could. You are now the one behind the controls"—has been the most difficult for us. How are parents supposed to know when the right time comes to let go? Young people are ready at a wide variety of ages. It is true that some of life's best lessons spring from your own mistakes, but sometimes the stakes are so high.

What if we decided *not* to let go now? Would she wrench away in rebellion? On the other hand, I remembered my childhood friend whose parents never let go. In her late thirties, she was still living in the same walk-through bedroom of their home, working as a teacher aide in the elementary school she had attended as a child.

We knew the boundaries had to be redrawn, but what should they become? We have always been better at doing than not doing, and not doing is what launching is all about. We expected her to responsibly take control of her life someday, and with a start, we realized that *someday* had come.

The decision made, we realized it was too momentous for casual assent. We needed to do something that would mark the moment in time. Something we could look back to as a "before" and "after." We needed to perform a ritual.

For two days we prepared. Buying things. Making things. Thinking things. On the morning of the event, we announced at breakfast that at 10:00 we would be conducting a ritual in the living room. By 9:30, both Karen and Laurel were waiting on the couch.

"Earlier this week," I addressed Karen, "you said that you never wanted to ask permission to do anything ever again. Dad and I have decided to grant that request. To commemorate your rite of passage into adulthood, we have prepared a ritual."

David presented her with a mylar balloon with long ribbons of red, blue, silver. On the balloon was a picture of a blissful Snoopy whose nose pointed to the sky, whose feet fluttered beneath him. "The balloon symbolizes your life," he said. "The ribbons are the controls. For years we have been the ones holding the ribbons—at first, very close to the balloon, but as you matured, we have let out the ribbons, little by little. Today we are giving the balloon to you."

I watched as David walked across the room and handed the balloon to Karen. Ready or not for all concerned, we had entered a new era of parenting.

I brought in a plaque with the Serenity Prayer and read it aloud. "God grant me the serenity to accept the things I cannot change, the courage to change the things I can; and the wisdom to know the difference" (Reinhold Niebuhr). I talked about tenacity and acceptance. I talked about giving life all you've got, while realizing that at times, walking away and beginning again is the best option of all. I talked about holding on and letting go.

We discussed the new boundaries. She would need to continue to ask to use the family car, but our decision would be based on if it was available, not on where she was going. She would need to let us know when she planned to be home, not as a curfew but out of courtesy.

David offered a prayer asking God to bless her as she made decisions in her life. For lunch, we had lasagna, as we always do on special occasions, and a cake decorated with a bunch of balloons iced across the top.

It was time to trust what we had done for nineteen years. Time to recognize the young woman she had become. Time to welcome a new adult into the ranks.

Gathering

NEW ANGLES

Sandra Doran

From the time my oldest son was young, I worried about his abilities in art. In nursery school, as all the other children at the easels painted large circles sporting eyes, noses, and mouths, my son lustily covered the entire canvas in sweeping red swaths. In kindergarten, when everybody else's kids brought home crafty pictures with carefully colored cutouts glued on, my son used the glue as a "medium" then dropped the paper on the way home and handed me something with pine needles stuck all over it. In elementary school, when other children created elaborate portraits with explicit bows, buttons, and ties, my son was still into stick figures. But my worries really began to intensify when his little brother came along.

Not only did this child like to draw, I soon discovered, but he delighted in details. At three, Jeff put ears and fingers and toes on his people. At five, he drew cars with mag wheels, racing stripes, exhaust headers, and spoilers. At six he sketched pterodactyls, pteranodons, stegosauri with intricate rows of plates.

As I watched my two sons, I became increasingly concerned about the day that the oldest would be hit by the difference in their artistic abilities. The moment, I knew, was inevitable. Eric would notice.

It happened on an overcast Sunday morning as I flurried around changing beds and folding towels. Striding past Jeff's room, I noticed him seated on the bed, his older brother holding open an encyclopedia as Jeff copied a detailed picture of a skeleton— clavicle, scapula, carpal bones, phalanges, femur, metatarsals. I sucked in my breath, knowing that this was the moment. If only I could think of an appropriate opening, I mused, I could find a way to remind my older son that talent comes in many shades and varieties. I stood in the shadow of the doorway ready to be The Good Mother, rehearsing the platitudes designed to Enhance Self-Esteem.

And then Eric spoke.

"I can't believe it, Mom," he said.

I sucked in my breath, braced myself.

"I can't believe it," he said again. "I'm only a kid, but *look* at what I'm getting *him* to do!"

I haven't spent a waking moment worrying about his self-esteem since.

Part of getting a handle on this whole thing called *parenthood,* I have learned, is releasing restricted expectations and discovering the uniqueness that each child has to offer. Since that morning of Eric's joyous announcement, he has revealed himself to indeed possess the gift of leading others along the road to accomplishment. When he discovered that his cousin, alone among the third grade class possessed a pair of shiny roller-blades that refused to stay on a straight and stable course, he commissioned himself to correct the situation. No matter that he, at the time, wobbled unsteadily when blades were strapped to his own fifth-grade feet. He knew the principles of roller-blading. He knew how to break things down. But more than that, he knew how to encourage.

My sister Holly and I settled ourselves on the couch before the open window as Eric approached Mallory, clinging to the brick wall in front of their house. The lesson began in the drive-way, the directions precise and assuring. "Bend your knees a little bit. It's OK. Just grab onto my arm."

And then, a little later, "OK. That's it. You've got it. Just relax now."

Still later, "OK, we're coming to the end of the driveway. Be careful. There's a little bump here."

The session continued all morning, into the afternoon, early evening, out of the driveway, onto the road, off the level, onto a hill. When I finally packed my kids and gear into the car at sunset and turned toward home, I looked into my rearview mirror one last time. Mallory appeared backlighted against the horizon, her small legs fluidly navigating the tar, her ponytail bobbing, her arms confidently swinging at her sides.

"She's good," Eric said with a smile. "She really caught on."

In the years that have followed, I have learned that when my own visual-spatial deficiency interferes with a task, there is one I can readily summon.

"I don't get it, Eric. How do you work this food processor?"

"This drawer's stuck. Something won't give."

"What is wrong with this can opener, anyway?"

Patiently, he repairs the breach, breaks down the steps, in-structs me on how to handle the situation should he be absent next time.

His talent for teaching, I am finding, has not gone unnoticed. Just last night, as we struggled through the capitals of the African countries for his seventh-grade social studies class, the telephone interrupted our homework session. "Can I speak with Eric?" came an adult voice. Quizzically, I handed him the receiver.

"Yes?" he said. "You can't figure out how to get out of Win-dows? Just a minute. Let me go up to my computer, and I'll help you."

As I sat at the table, tapping my pencil and reviewing the six pages of homework yet to conquer, Eric's voice sounded from above, assuring his friend's mother not to worry, that indeed, sooner or later she would get the hang of her new computer.

Fifteen minutes later, we resumed the battle of the school-work. Reading aloud the directions, I shuddered for a minute. "Draw the garments worn by your favorite African tribe."

Don't hold it against him, I silently entreated the teacher, as Eric sharpened his pencil for the task. My son may not be ready for the Metropolitan Museum of Art, but should there be a future Michelangelo looking for a teacher to guide him to greatness, let me know. I've got just the kid.

Gathering

THANKFULNESS

Dale Slongwhite

"You pray different than me," Laurel called from the end of the driveway.

I was standing half-in/half-out of the kitchen door sending her off to kindergarten with a wave. I waited for her to continue, which, of course, she did.

"I say, 'Thank you, thank you, thank you,'" she said, "and you say, 'Help me, help me, help me.'" Having accurately assessed my prayer life, she turned and skipped up the street, lime-green backpack and curly red pigtails bobbing.

I have spent many years pondering the wisdom of my five-year-old. And I have to admit, even though I know prayer is intended to serve more than one purpose, sometimes I get stuck in one necessary facet—that of asking for help. So just for a moment, I'm going to meditate on some of the things for which I am thankful.

I'm thankful for life.

I was working on the second floor of the administration building of the college when I heard the screech of tires on pavement, crunch of metal against metal, and then nothing. Trembling, I joined a group descending the stairs and hurrying to the front door. "I don't know why I'm doing this," I told a co-worker. "Twenty-four years ago I stood on this very corner and watched a man die before the ambulance got here." And then: "That's *my* car!" I took off running toward the three-car pileup, searching for Karen.

"You're lucky," the tow-truck driver said. "The wheel took the brunt of the force. If the impact had been just a few inches forward, the windshield would have shattered and the side of the car would have squashed at least half the seat your daughter was sitting in."

The next morning my sister Holly gave birth to Cooper Finley David. As soon as we heard the news, we jumped into our one functional vehicle and drove 100 miles to the hospital. Boys are a rare phenomenon in our family, and we had to see him firsthand.

When my daughter's turn to hold the new baby came, I watched Cooper stare at Karen intently, as if asking, "Who are you, and what are you doing here?" Good question from he who was only eight hours into his journey of life to she who was only twenty-four hours from almost ending hers. Somehow all the working parts of a newborn baby reminded me anew of the miracle of life. How beginning it and ending it and sustaining it are all in the hands of God.

In the aftermath, I've decided that I don't want to die too soon. Not because I fear death but because I enjoy life. Despite all the pollution, pain, and poverty, I still think the time sandwiched between birth and death is a gift from God—a gift of time He would like us to explore and examine and marvel at as if each day were being unwrapped for the very first time. Because in reality, it is.

I'm thankful for the days of my childhood.

I suppose I lived through winters in my childhood, but I only remember the summers. Summer *Sundays* actually—hundreds of them clasping hands to embrace an entire childhood, sunny, salty, and safe. Every Sunday when the weather allowed, our family drove to Groton, Connecticut, and loaded ourselves and our paraphernalia into a sixteen-foot motorboat moored to a short dock in a narrow inlet. The hand-painted sign crookedly fastened to a post in the channel between the docks said *NO WAKE*, so Dad obediently paddled past the Boston Whalers, past the cabin cruisers. When we reached the farthest end of the docks where the ladies in lawn chairs waved pleasantly from the decks of yachts, he'd pull violently on the cord to start the Evinrude. We'd putt past the sailboats bobbing in unison with the tide, their turnbuckles clanking against metal booms. And finally, with nothing but expansive sea before us, Dad would open up the Evinrude to full throttle, and we'd be off—ponytails flying at perpendicular angles to our heads, bouncing in the wake of other boats, sheets of water pouring over the sides drenching us, laughing and squinting in the bright sunlight.

Standing at the helm, ruddy round face beaming, captain of all he surveyed, my father allowed the stress of his small machine-shop business to be borne away in the salt breeze with one gigantic "AAAH! *This* is the life." He'd lift his Greek fisherman's cap, rub his head, and he'd ask, "Isn't this something, girls?" Every Sunday, "Isn't this something?" Sandy, Holly, Mom, and I would nod vigorously. It really *was* something—the throaty squawk of circling seagulls, the rhythmic dong-dong-dong of bell buoys rolling in swells, the blinding sparkle of sunlight glinting off waves.

I'm thankful for those days of my childhood. They have served as a good foundation upon which to build a life.

I'm thankful for Divine intervention.

"Dale, by any chance are you looking for a job?"

White-knuckled, I gripped the receiver. At 7:50 a.m. on that Monday morning, I'd been heading for the shower when the distinct impression came to me, "The phone is going to ring, and you need to talk to the caller." I knew the voice, so I put down my towel and waited. By 8:10 when the phone hadn't rung, I thought wires had been crossed somewhere, and I picked up the towel and headed to the bathroom. Before I made it there, the phone rang.

"Actually," I said to the employer I'd left nearly three years before, "I *am* looking for a job."

"Jim!" he cried to my other ex-boss, "she's looking for a job!" And to me, "Will you come in to talk to us? Do you have time today?"

"Tomorrow," I said, but I already knew I was going to take it.

Late Friday afternoon, we'd been to see a financial counselor who said our monetary picture was grim. I had to return to the full-time work force immediately, he said, and if we were to stay afloat, I had to earn more than I'd ever earned in my life. He sighed and looked at me, his face conveying doubt either in my ability to do so or to do it quickly.

I had just completed a bachelor's degree in communications, and I wanted to leave secretarial behind for something more reflective of my talents. To enter a new profession, I'd have to start at the bottom and work up; in secretarial, my experience would guarantee a top job. I didn't want to be a secretary anymore, but when the phone rang first thing Monday morning after I felt impressed to listen, listen I did.

"There's something you don't know," Jim said the next day during the interview. "We've added a Communications Department since you left. We knew you got your degree, and you probably don't want to be a secretary anymore, so we went to the VP in charge of Communications and asked, 'If Dale comes back, can we get her into some writing?' She said sure. So, Dale, if you'll help us out of a jam and come back as our secretary, we'll get you a college student as an assistant, and you can get involved in some writing. What do you think?"

"How much are you going to pay me for this?" I asked. They laughed then stated a sum which was a notable increase over my earnings of three years prior.

I called the financial advisor the next day to let him know God had worked it all out, and in less than two weeks, I was working.

I'm thankful for the minute details of creation.

I'm not a bird watcher, but David is. For twenty-five years, he's been tracking birds with the same binoculars and bird book I gave him as a gift the first year we were married. What *I* like is quietness, a slowed pace, no expectations on me, the sound and feel of my own measured breath, sun on my face. So I've accompanied David into the woods, onto the dunes, through the fields, and beside the river banks many times over the years. And I've got this to say about birds: I can't believe how many varieties there are.

"I'd say nine or ten inches," David said, binoculars to his eyes. "He's got a yellow belly. The top of his head is black-and-white."

We were in a park built around a sea theme in the Yucatan Peninsula, but David was looking into a tree that just happened to be there. I was sitting on the pavement with the bird book open before me. I'd ventured into the middle of Boston to buy a book on Mexican birds as a gift to him before we left on vacation. "Any yellow on the head?" I asked.

"Yes!" he said with excitement. "A little patch."

"Great kiskadee," I informed him, took a deep breath, looked up into the great blue sky and around me at unfamiliar terrain, closed my eyes, and felt at peace.

In Arizona we spotted three varieties of hummingbirds: the Rufous hummingbird, the black-chinned hummingbird, the broad-tailed hummingbird. On a freezing day in Maine, we watched jet-black cormorants glide low across the sea, arch their s-shaped necks, dive beneath the waves, and surface yards from where they'd gone under. Once I embarrassed David in front of a group of serious birders by looking through his spotting scope at a snowy owl and asking, "How do you know it isn't a seagull?"

I've watched with interest the return of great blue herons to New England. I can spot a red-tailed hawk in a tree at a great distance. I've snuck up on pelicans in Florida. I've taken a flying leap onto a boat we almost missed on its way to the bird sanctuary island of Contoy off the coast of Cancun. On the island, we saw dozens upon dozens of soaring brown boobys and hundreds of male frigatebirds inflating large red pouches on their necks in hopes of attracting a mate. Last week's newspaper reported two endangered species wintering nearby: a peregrine falcon on a church steeple and a bald eagle on a riverbank. I'm sure we'll be searching for them soon, and I look forward to it.

Add a stripe, fork the tail, curve the bill, lengthen the legs, and you've got another bird species. I'm in awe of the God who thought them all up and thankful that He did.

Today I got an e-mail from Laurel who's away at college. "Opened my PO box today," she wrote, "and there was the application to work at the Lowell Park this summer. Start praying cuz we always seem to get serious answers . . ."

Do I detect a "Help me, help me, help me"?

Gathering

RAYS

Sandra Doran

There is something exhilarating about stealing a beach day in September. Walking unabashedly past closed entrance booths with signs that read "Local residents only," stepping onto a mile of sand dotted by just a few stray blankets, unfolding a beach chair and opening a library book while my sons cavort in the waves, I am a fugitive from winter—on the lam from cold, dark gray days that surely will never come—a recipient of grace.

Settling into my chair, I am reminded of the children's book *Frederick* that entertained my two boys in years past. As fellow mice work gathering corn, nuts, wheat, and straw for the approaching winter, Frederick is caught sitting quietly apart from the group.

"Frederick," the laboring mice query, the artist's depiction showing them with corncobs held high above their heads as they march by, "why don't you work?"

"I do work," he replies. "I gather sun rays for the cold dark days."

Later when Frederick is found staring out at a meadow, the question is repeated. He answers. "I gather colors, for winter is gray."

Finally, Frederick is discovered almost half-asleep. "Are you dreaming?" his fellow mice want to know.

"Oh no," he responds. "I'm gathering words. For the winter days are long and many, and we'll run out of things to say."

This September day, I gather images, inspirations, insight. Surveying the fortunate few scattered before the glittering Atlantic, I discover four children on the beach this bright and wind-laden afternoon. Each has found some treasure worth the whole of his attention. Two little fellows find dignity in the discards of humanity—a paper cup, an old brown bag, a can, a bottle. An afternoon is devoted to their labor—filling the cup with sand, emptying it into the bag, shaking it around, transferring it to the bottle, the can.

Down the beach a middle-sized boy walks. His afternoon's find is a stick as big around as a loaf of French bread, half his own height in length. It is a horse to ride, a fencer's foil, an artist's brush on a wet sand palette.

In the foreground walks a girl, her feet making trails on the fine sand. She stoops for a moment and scoops up a handful of gravel and broken shells, sifting them out through her fingers, enjoying the feel of their smooth transit, the music of their softly clinked song.

I sit on the high edge of the sloping sands and feel a sort of holy contentment. For woven through the golden seascape of wind and children runs a theme, Godlike in its origin, glimmering with a reminder of Eden, glistening with a hint of the New Jerusalem. With each fluid movement of tanned fingers, each shake of a cup, each tap of a stick, work and art and play are inextricably bound up into one powerful whole. Time has ceased to exist for the four children who ply their trades with nature's wares. They are fulfilled with the sacredness of purpose; they are content with the wholesomeness of play; they are complete with the uniqueness of creation.

I put aside the untouched book on my lap, for before me plays a message I may never catch again. We have been created in the image of God—created to work, to play, to build. And when our whole being is bound up, radiantly, in all three—when our working becomes playing, our playing, creating—then we are approaching the very borders of heaven itself.

Children innately understand the perfect juxtaposition of the three. It is only as adults that we categorize, designating our days for work, our evenings for play, and if we are lucky, catching a few spontaneous moments for creation.

Perhaps the bliss of Eden, the sweet appeal of the hereafter, lies in the fact that we will work—not to put food in our bellies, shelter over our heads, clothes on our backs—but for the sheer pleasure of it, for the fresh awareness of a job well done, the honest joy of a day's creation. And in the measured grace of our planting, the sure tempo of our sowing, will be the artist's song of existence.

For today, I draw joy and insight from the industrious hands shaping sand, the free-spirited minds conceiving turreted castles, the busy legs running to tide pools for buckets of water. Hailing my youngest son who is emerging from the waves with a radiant smile, I begin to smooth away a long, flat rectangle of wet sand.

He is nine now; too soon he will leave sand-castling behind for the sophistication of surfing and deep-sea fishing. Just for to-day I can sit, a young boy as my cover, and dig past layers of fine, loose sand into beds of hard-packed grit, strata of darker granules, until the very ocean itself begins to ooze upward into my hands. I can dig deeper while the sand becomes as soft as silt, the ocean seeps back into the ground, leaving only a trace of white minerals behind. I can pack hard layers of sand into a cup, over-turn it and twist my wrist with just the right amount of pressure, surround my chasm with mighty walls. I can find bird feathers, small sticks, tiny stones, and decorate my fortress like no other.

And when I return home, fulfilled from the simple act of creation, the joy of work and play and artistic endeavor, I can remember to face my tasks with renewed vision. I can add a sprig of parsley to a pasta salad, plant my chrysanthemums with an eye to symmetry, work on a course syllabus with a fine sense of balance, planning independent assignments, group projects, and presentations with art and precision. I can enter the fall with vigor and promise, live through the winter with inner warmth, find new ways to blend working and playing and creating into one, and then, when summer comes again, make of ordinary sand the sacredness of clay.

Gathering

SILVER

Dale Slongwhite

We journeyed to the elite coastal tourist town of Watch Hill, Rhode Island, because I like to ride carousels. Rumor had it they had a famous one that's been in operation since the 1880s, making it the oldest carousel in the country. It sits high on a cliff overlooking the ocean in a bend in the road that separates the downtown from the summer mansions of the wealthy. Last winter, a local artist repainted each horse and displayed the finished masterpieces in the local library before remounting them in the carousel in the spring.

I was excited as David slipped into a parking place in front of the souvenir, ice-cream, and beachwear shops and the familiar carousel tune wafted through the salty evening air. We spotted an opening between other adults circling the "flying horses" and stepped up for a peek before purchasing my ticket. It was then that we discovered that whoever had told us about the carousel had failed to mention one important detail.

True, the horses were spectacular with their shiny lacquered finishes, leather saddles, and real-hair manes. Unfortunately, this was a "kids only" carousel, since the horses were smaller than the norm. The miniature horses, legs posed in galloping style, swung by chains mounted high up beneath the carousel's roof. Disappointed, I lingered awhile and studied the enamored faces of the lucky little ones who got to ride the horses round and round, reach for the brass and silver rings held by the mechanical arm, and be transported by the cheerful beat of the music.

Later, strolling on the boardwalk alongside the harbor, licking a chocolate-almond ice-cream cone, gaping at million-dollar yachts and sailboats, I noticed a boy of about five sitting on a wooden bench. He was swinging his legs and chatting happily with his father. "I got six silver rings," he said proudly. "I held on tight and reached way out." He demonstrated by clinging to his father's arm and stretching out over the bench, his face animated with the memory.

Staring absently out to sea, the father answered in an unimpressed monotone. "Silver rings don't matter," he said. "Only the brass ones count. Then you get a free ride."

The boy's legs stopped their carefree swinging. His brow furrowed in question. He stared at his father's face, trying to figure out the significance of the words, and in that moment, I hoped he never would. I hoped he never got so caught up with building his career, paying his bills, repairing his home, changing the oil in his car, that the simple joy he experienced that evening dimmed, faded, and eventually dissolved.

I glanced at the father and wondered what he had been through that rendered him so cynical and if I should stop and set him straight. Maybe he had spent years reaching for the brass ring, disappointed at retrieving a silver one, not realizing he *had* grasped a prize. Didn't he know that silver rings matter as much as brass ones? The anticipation matters. The preparing matters. The reaching at just the right moment matters. The grasping matters. The smooth feel of the metal matters. The storing of the rings on the horse's ears matters. The tossing of the rings into the purple plastic pail held by the attendant as the horses slow down matters.

If you carry the logic of the father to its fullest, why bother riding a wooden horse at all? You aren't going to get anywhere. If you carry my logic to the fullest, the process is as important as the prize. The learning as valuable as the diploma. The enjoyment of work as fulfilling as the paycheck at week's end. The feeling of pride in participating as satisfying as the winning. The recognition of the little reasons to be happy as heartwarming as attaining the worked-for goal. The rejoicing in God's daily gift of life as exhilarating as walking through the pearly gates. The making time in the now as high a priority as marking time for the future.

Slowly I regained my rhythm of stepping carefully on the boardwalk's crosswise planks, of licking the melting spots on my cone, of listening to the seagull's squawks, of feeling the salty breeze on my cheeks, of enjoying the companionship of my husband.

David and I strolled on into the darkness, and I never knew for sure how the father-son drama played itself out. In a way, I regretted not putting in my two cents, but they didn't need me . . . they needed each other. One to mentor successful navigation of the adult world and one to be an anchor point of innocent wonder.

A last glance over my shoulder gave me hope that perhaps the father *had* gotten his first clue about the importance of process from the expression on his son's face. The next move would need to be his.

Gathering

HOPE

Sandra Doran

The raspberries tasted wonderful—sweet and tart at the same time, a deep, juicy flavor, much more distinctive than strawberries, I decided. I was just licking one last, lone fragment from the side of the cup when Marian made her casual announcement.

"You know John may have sprayed these bushes with something poisonous. We could probably die. It would serve us right for eating the berries when he's not home."

I dropped the cup and looked up at her, feeling suddenly woozy, as if the poison had already started taking effect. "I guess I'd better get going," I said. "I told my mother I'd be back in an hour."

The next few days dragged out in silent agony. I wondered how long it would be before I could be sure that the poison hadn't entered my system. When I crawled into bed each night, I mentally calculated how many hours it had been since I'd eaten the berries. By the third day I figured I was safe. But the damage had already been done. For the first time in my ten years of living I had come face to face with my own mortality. And the idea was not easily discarded.

I knew, now, that although I probably wouldn't die within the next few days of acute raspberry poisoning, my time would eventually come. I would not go on forever, always running up and down the fields of Lucas Park Road, caught in a state of perpetual youth.

With this disconcerting awareness came a gripping fear of the passing of time, the fleeting sweetness of childhood. I confided in my mother one evening, sitting down beside her on the back steps as she husked corn for supper. "The days are going by so fast. Sometimes it makes me feel afraid."

My gentle mother put aside the piece of corn she was preparing, its green leaves pulled halfway down the cob. Her face was understanding, yet hopeful. She thought for a moment then replied. "Perhaps if you had something special to look forward to, it wouldn't bother you so much."

I nodded, searching for a clue in her words, some answer that would stop the heavy weight of the relentless wheel of time spinning in my head.

Brushing pieces of silk from her skirt, Mom stood up and entered the house. When she returned, she held in her hand a cereal box. On the back was a photograph of a doll, her face framed by a mass of shining gold hair. She wore a red-checkered shirt and denim jeans with a small rope belt. Her name was Calico Lassie.

We carefully poured the cereal out of the box and into a plastic container. Then, with scissors, we removed the mailing label. With a steady hand I printed in the data: Miss Sandra Finley, 57 Lucas Park Road, Norwich, CT 06360. I slipped the order into an envelope, and thus the waiting period began.

Although the box unequivocally stated, "Please allow 4-6 weeks for delivery," I took up my vigil before the picture window by the end of the first week, anxiously racing to the mailbox each time I saw the blue-and-white mail jeep round the bend. Four weeks passed then five. And then, just when I had about given up, just when I'd decided six weeks might as well be translated "Forever," the mail carrier slipped something into the box that looked suspicious, something long and narrow, something wrapped in brown paper, something that made the passing of time infinitely worth it.

It has been a long time since I looked on Calico Lassie's face, touched her shining hair, breathed in her new-doll smell. And while she had the power to quell my childhood fears, she could not stop the relentless turning of the wheel of time. Years have flown past in a whirl of color since my days on Lucas Park Road. Decades that have brought me two children of my own, boys full of their own joys, dreams, and probing questions. My thirteen-year-old confided in me recently, as I bustled about the house, tidying rooms on a Sunday morning, "Time is going by too fast. I don't like it."

I put down the pile of mail that I was sorting and looked at this boy whose inner hopes and fears were really no different from my own. I told him about John's raspberries, the unhusked piece of corn placed on the back step, the emptied cereal box, the six-week vigil before the bay window, the oblong package that made my heart race with anticipation. I told him that I have learned that when there is something to look forward to, the passing of time can be a cause for rejoicing rather than fear.

Carefully, he emptied the cereal from the box into the plastic container. With steady hand, he printed "Eric Doran, 10 Redgate Road ... " Today he waits, at the threshold of a new millennium, for a round disk that will send sound and images into a machine that did not even exist in my dreams as I lay in my bed on Lucas Park Road. But although the content of his package is radically different from the prize I awaited in the 1960s, his fragile, hopeful spirit is no different from my own.

The wheel spins. Time whirls in an unremitting stream of lights and darks, sound and silence, todays and tomorrows. But I have learned that when there is something to look forward to, the passing of time can be a cause for rejoicing rather than fear. And when I stop to think about it, there is something special ahead, something awaiting all who believe, something ordered especially for us by a loving Parent. Something as different from my limited, human understanding as a compact disc to a child of the sixties. And I have a suspicion that had I caught even the tiniest fraction of a glimpse of it back in the days of the raspberries, I would have considered Calico Lassie mere child's play.

Gathering

FRIENDS

Dale Slongwhite

As far as I could see in any direction, flat green and brown fields extended to the horizon. Some were dotted with cows grazing beside their calves or sows nursing their litters. Way off in the distance, a miniature puff of dirt marked a plowing tractor. Ahead of us stretched a road so straight it appeared God Himself had bent down with a ruler to draw it. For hours we passed only isolated houses, an occasional small town, a tractor-trailer hauling a double load. Billboards succinctly captured the scene: "Dairy Queen, 55 miles ahead."

"So," I said. "Anything exciting happen to you in kindergarten?"

Georgia laughed. Four mornings earlier, we two thirty-something women had pulled out of my driveway in northeastern Massachusetts and headed west. Six months before, her husband and children had driven across the country to begin new jobs and schools and she had stayed behind to sell the house. At long last, papers had passed, and she'd asked me to help drive her home.

For 1,500 miles now, we had talked and laughed and reminisced about the good times our families had shared—paddling canoes across a glasslike lake at dawn in Vermont and spotting a beaver, camping at the site of the last wolf's den in Connecticut, playing games around our kitchen table or in their basement family room, battling Class 3 rapids in upstate New York with the canoe wedging around a rock, singing rounds and ditties as she played the guitar. But now it seemed as if we had said it all, and still nearly one thousand miles lay between us and our destination.

"What about you?" Georgia asked. "Tell me about the dreams of your youth. What did you always want to do?" And so with no meals to cook, no house to clean, no job to manage, no children or husband to assist, in a red Hyundai Excel pointing due west, surrounded by terrain foreign to a New Englander, I began to explore my dreams because a friend asked me to.

"I've always wanted to write," I said. Thus began a ten-year journey of classes, experimentation of words on paper, attendance at conferences and seminars.

Friends have always been an important part of my life. In elementary school, I gathered with Mary Anne and Joe and Colleen each afternoon around an oil spot in a corner of the school yard attempting to knock a shiny silver ballbearing out of the center with our cat-eye agates. In junior high, Pam and I spent hours trying to compose a letter to Murray the K, a radio disc jockey on 1010 WINS New York, explaining why he should arrange for us to meet the Beatles.

Friends have helped define who I am. With them and through them, I have gained an understanding of various facets of life.

I met Maureen when I was fourteen. "*Are you Dale Finley?*" she asked, serving my food in the camp cafeteria.

"Yes," I said.

"I thought so," she answered, her voice tinged with sarcasm.

That afternoon I found out she liked a particular young man who liked me. Later, when we both had no use for him, we forged a friendship that has lasted over thirty years. She wore the first pair of pantyhose I ever saw. "What *are* those things?" I asked, admiring her as a woman on the cutting edge of fashion. Over the years, we have written, e-mailed, met for dinner when she's in town, and with great pleasure, befriended each other's grown children.

I cherish my friends and have worked hard to keep relationships alive. Deby has been hard to hang onto in adulthood, but I've never let go. We joined a public-speaking group when we were sixteen and spoke in many churches in Connecticut, Massachusetts, and Rhode Island. We wrote sermons together, swapped clothes, prayed, and engaged in countless discussions on the meaning of life. A sincere teenager who put a great deal of effort into life, she has had more than her share of difficulties. There have been many moves and much upheaval, yet she remains strong and optimistic, moving ahead, growing, accomplishing great things.

A few years ago, I ran into numerous dead ends trying to contact Deby. When I finally reached her phone machine, I made an impulsive decision. "I'm flying to see you for the weekend," I said. "Will you pick me up at the airport?" She did, and for forty-eight hours we talked all day and late into the night—about her recent divorce, the upcoming weddings of our daughters, our struggles for a degree, our search for a deeper spiritual life.

With friends, I have plotted the future, examined the past, bounced around ideas, swapped recipes and empathy, searched for truth, made sense of my journey.

Jeanne and I roomed together our freshman year in college. "You probably think I was mad at you a lot this year," I said in May. "But really, there was only one time."

"I know what it was," she interrupted. "The time I broke the sink and you kept forgetting and turning on the water."

"I forgot about that," I said. "I was mad then too."

"It had to be the time about the laundry, right?" she asked.

"No," I said. "I forgot about that. I *was* mad then."

Unwittingly, Jeanne reminded me of numerous times she had raised my ire over the past eight months and it took me several days to calm down. I did and haven't been mad at her since. In an uncanny way, the events of our adult lives have paralleled each other. We have been poor at the same time. We have lived in small houses near family at the same time. We both have strong bonds with our sisters. Our husbands returned to school in their thirties, and we wives anticipated positive results. Instead, within weeks of each other, our spouses accepted jobs in high-cost-of-living areas, and we each sold our home only to acquire an impossible mortgage on another. The phone calls flew back and forth between New Jersey and Boston as we struggled to find meaning and hope in our complementary situations. If one of us could make it, the other knew she could too.

Be it pain or pleasure, fear or joy, I have shared it with friends.

I met Donna when we returned to school to wrap up our degrees at age forty. We were kindred spirits—women who had raised families and were now eager to develop our dormant, creative talents. She introduced me to her theory of "Pockets of Pleasure" that changed my life.

"I don't expect my home to be perfect," she told me. "Instead, in different little places, I design groupings of pictures or something that makes me happy every time I look at it."

My current pockets of pleasure include a windowbox shaped like a boat, a bouquet of silk tulips on my front door, and a dozen black-and-white photos I developed and grouped on the walls of my stairway.

Friends from schools I have attended, friends from churches where we've been members, friends from neighborhoods where we have lived, friends from jobs where I have worked—together we have celebrated milestones, encouraged each other in disappointments, rejoiced at accomplishments, laughed at the hilarity of life, made sense of the confusion, shared a history. Over meals, through telephone wires, tramping through forests or city blocks, traveling in cars, standing in church foyers, sitting on couches in living rooms, or most recently via e-mail, we have talked of marriage, of birth, of infertility, of returning to college, of finances, of AIDS, of homes, of divorce, of careers, of moves, of children's weddings, of Alzheimer's, of grandchildren, of abuse, of God, of hopes dashed, of dreams grasped.

Friends have structured my life, given meaning to my life, challenged my life, filled my life with adventure. For all of it, I thank them.

Gathering

PERSPECTIVE

Sandra Doran

On my first day as a student in fifteen years, I laid my hand down on the desk and plunged my wrist into a wad of gray gum, entwining my watch band with a web of gossamer threads. "Welcome back to school," a twenty-something sitting beside me offered with a cynical smile. The stickiness of my initiation aside, I entered into my doctoral classes with relish, imbibing theory and practics with an interest borne of intellectual curiosity and a lifelong love of learning. In reading, studying, and creating text I felt accomplished, confident, stimulated . . . until the late fall afternoon in "Disorders of Cognition" when Professor Clinton called me to the front of the class.

I had established myself as a student of note in his class, keeping up with readings, taking a key role in class discussions, presenting watertight theoretical arguments. But on this particular afternoon, Professor Clinton was not interested in theory alone.

"When working with students who present with mental challenges," he said, "it is important to analyze a task into its component parts. If a student has difficulty, continue to split the task into smaller and smaller parts, until you can find a point at which the student is comfortable learning. Then proceed forward from there."

I nodded, appreciating as always his clear, simple logic. His next words made my heart freeze.

"Let's illustrate this point now. Ms. Doran, do you know how to tie a necktie?"

I swallowed, knowing that I was about to be exposed. Ask me to do anything with language—write an encyclopedia entry on plant reproduction, interpret the meaning of Plato's *Republic,* deliver a speech to the White House staff. Ask me to teach a child, encourage an adult, develop a meaningful relationship with a senior citizen. Ask me to think, feel, conceptualize, understand. But don't ask me to do.

"Not exactly," I managed slowly.

"Perfect," he said. "Would you step to the front of the room, please?"

Heart pounding, I slowly extricated my body from my seat, acutely aware of the eyes of fellow doctoral students glued to my every move. During the long, measured walk to the front of the room, I felt the heaviness of a lifetime of practical ineptness weighing on every step.

The first time I ever attempted to bake a cake, I interpreted the word *instant* on the box to mean that all that was necessary was to open the package, pour the powder into a pan, and slide it into the oven. The first time I ever got behind the wheel of a car, my mother yelled frantically, "Get to the side of the road!"

"Which side?" I asked.

Directions eluded me, schematics confounded, explanations baffled. I had made it through life by the good graces of a father who constructed my science projects, a husband who changed the ink cartridge on my printer, a vocabulary that landed me jobs in places that did not rely on manual dexterity. And now, in the very environment that fostered my strengths, I was being asked to expose my weakness.

Somehow I managed to stand beside Professor Clinton, face the expectant class, move my frozen fingers in imitation of his own, request further clarification when I could not grasp a simple step. What I remember most clearly about that afternoon is his patient, reassuring voice. "If this is too much for you to handle at once, we can back up one more step." Back up we did. It's a wonder we didn't end up at the historical inauguration of the first necktie christened in France.

Two years later, I rush into the house fresh out of a traffic jam, prepared to gather up my oldest son, his trumpet, his music, his brother, and rapidly transport all of us to the middle-school gymnasium for the spring band concert. I am met at the door by a frantic, demanding voice. "Where were you? We've got to get going. We're going to be late. I don't have a white shirt to wear. Where does Dad keep his ties?"

Ties. I freeze in my tracks. "You have to wear a tie, Eric?"

Nodding, he throws three white shirts aside. "These stupid things don't even fit me anymore, and it's almost 6:15. We've got to get going!"

Kicking the shirts aside, I offer him a dress shirt of his father's—size 35 sleeve. Puffing and folding over his wrists, the garment looks like some new style invented for the small man with an inflated ego. Eric adds it to the pile on the floor. "I'm not going," he says.

One last trip through his closet and I locate a shirt with one button missing, mercifully below the point of the tuck-in. He dons the shirt, selects a red paisley tie from his father's collection, and begins wrapping. And then comes the inevitable. "I don't know how to tie this stupid thing," he shouts in exasperation. "Can you do it?"

I pray that his father will burst through the front door, his out-of-town meeting unexpectedly canceled. I pray that the church treasurer will pull into the driveway, the neighbor across the street will decide it is time to walk his dog. I need a man. Any man.

"You'll have to get the band teacher to tie it," I call from the

front window where I have spotted not even a male dog travers-
ing the street in front of the house.

"The band teacher? I'll look like an idiot. I'm not going."

Somehow I sweep him into the car, trumpet, music stand,
brother jammed into the back seat. "Send me a man, Lord," I pray,
scanning the sides of the road for likely prospects.

In the school parking lot we pull up beside somebody's grandfather. There, against the rear bumper, away from the prying eyes
of junior-high tormentors, Eric hands him the offending piece of
apparel, and this random man, placed on earth, I am sure at this
moment, for this purpose alone, does the job. We enter the school
building, smoothing collars, cowlicks, jagged nerves. Eric disap-
pears behind the stage. Fifteen minutes later he files out with his
schoolmates, appearing from my third-row vantage point like a
freshly pressed, formal, handsome, young, composed adolescent.
He takes his place in the brass section. Readies his trumpet. Adds
his sound to violins, flutes, timpani, French horns.

Toward the middle of the program, five boys are called by
name. Eric Doran . . . Robert Delucia . . . They step forward. Lift
their golden instruments to their lips. Produce a melody that
makes hearts soar and feet tap.

I sit in a folding chair, consumed by the sound, inspired by
the rousing, glorious beat. And I know then that we are all a study
in complexity, a complicated bundle of strengths and weaknesses,
novice and expert, rough and polished. I, who cannot tie a tie, he
who is eluded by a seventh-grade social studies text, his father
who can preach but not spell, his brother who can spell but not
wait. Bound by our limitations, we shine out in moments of glory,
lift one another above the constraints of narrow human vision.

The boys blow out one last long note. Lower their trumpets.
Bow their heads in a flushed finish. The audience claps wildly.
Eric Doran resumes his place somewhere behind the woodwinds.
And the band plays on.

Gathering

IDENTITY

Dale Slongwhite

I have just finished wrapping the gift of empowerment for Laurel for Christmas. It is a hammer—tightly bound in layers of pink tissue and camouflaged in a shirt box covered with red holiday paper. On Christmas morning Laurel will open it, furrow her brow, and upon remembering, she will laugh and then cry. And when she returns to college for second semester, she'll pack the hammer to hang the poster she'll be receiving from us and the collage of cat photos Karen has assembled.

I had a hard time finding the hammer. David doesn't keep a neat workbench. But after rummaging around on top and opening a few drawers, I spotted it beneath a few other well-used tools. It looks pretty good for sixteen years old—the foot-long oak handle still lacquered and shiny with just a few dings and paint stains, the steel head still solidly attached and only slightly discolored.

On Mother's Day, when Karen was two and a half and Laurel was almost one, David hauled several sheets of plywood into the tiny backyard of our condominium and went to work with saw and hammer. "I'm making a gift for you," he said, and every time I passed the sliding glass doors in the living room, I looked out, analyzed the progress, and made a guess. "A bookcase?" I asked.

"A shelf? A table?" Intent in his work, he never looked up. Just smiled and shook his head.

A large box took shape . . . 8 feet x 8 feet, I'd guess . . . with sides about a foot high. Then he nailed triangular-shaped pieces of wood in two corners like, like seats. "It looks," I said, hesitating, puzzled. "It looks like a sandbox . . ." My voice trailed off in disappointment.

Why did he think a gift to the children was a gift to me? Did he think of me now only as a mother with no identity of her own, just an extension of the children, or they of me, so that a gift for them counted somehow as a gift to me?

Long into that summer and the next as the girls baked sand cookies and sifted and built by the hour and I watched from a lounge chair with a book or through the sliding glass doors while vacuuming, I thought of his reply and thanked him again and again. "My gift to you," he said, "is not this sandbox. It is the time you will have when the girls are contentedly playing." We had no way of knowing that that gift of time would extend from preschool play into a college dormitory many years later.

Just before Karen started kindergarten, we moved across town to our first home, and the sandbox came with us. It was chipped and scratched, so David covered the forest green paint with a fresh coat of fire-engine red. For several more years, the girls dug and raked, molded and formed, until gradually they felt too old for "baby" play. When the sandbox had lain dormant for a year, I suggested we cart it off to the dump. Instead, David brought home pallets from his job in the warehouse, set them beside the sandbox, and bought each of his daughters a hammer.

We're not talking a toy hammer or a cheap hammer. We're talking a genuine tool purchased in a real hardware store. A tool a contractor would be proud to use. A hammer with a solid wood handle a foot long that weighed at least four pounds. A hammer I wondered if they could pick up, and if they did, would they kill themselves or someone else. And beyond that, I wondered what interest my daughters would have in a hammer anyway when they were having fun with dolls and tea sets in the house.

Remarkably, no one was injured, and Karen and Laurel became quite adept and confident with their hammers. For two summers, they and a host of neighborhood boys and girls used one end of the hammers to rip apart the sandbox, nail by nail, board by board, and the other end to pound those same nails back into those same boards, although now in a different shape. Little by little, they transformed the sandbox into a clubhouse with four sides, a floor, a roof, and a door that wedged closed and dropped open. Sometimes the group sat in the clubhouse with a flashlight and talked. Mostly, they just worked on it with the hammers.

When Karen was eleven and Laurel was ten, we moved to another state, and the clubhouse stayed behind. The hammers merged in with the household tools. Play was different here. Girls weren't into tools. Boys didn't play with girls. Activities were more gender-specific or gender-attracting. Difficult days followed as Karen and Laurel learned to resist yet navigate this strange new land where gender roles were more defined.

Except for occasional uses when it was chosen over another, the hammer lay idle for more than a decade. After Christmas, it will go to college. And I hope that as Laurel pounds in the nails for her new poster and collage, she will remember those long summer afternoons ripping apart a sandbox and constructing a clubhouse. Afternoons when the seed was planted that she was an empowered woman who could choose to play with dolls or wield a hammer or do both.

Gathering

WINS AND LOSSES

Sandra Doran

I couldn't always sit like this and play Monopoly with my sons. Such a luxury is borne of years of practice, endless tests of patience, storms ridden out and battles won.

When I was a child, games took center stage in my home on Lucas Park Road. Two weeks after we moved in, Dad began nailing plywood shelves on the wall of the furnace room for our growing collection of rectangular boxes with plastic pieces. In the eight years that we lived there, the shelves took over the furnace room, and the boxes took over the shelves, spilling over the sides, wedged at curious angles, enticing us with promised challenges.

We wheeled plastic cars, peopled by family members, in the game of Life. We boggled and scrabbled. Flipped over cards and rolled dice. Spun wheels and hid rubbery creatures in cabins. Assembled large puzzle pieces as we sought to conquer the world. Stuck eyes and legs and antennae into plastic bugs. Slapped our palms onto yellow plastic hands. Toppled towers of colored blocks. Sent people back to start. Passed "Go." Changed tires in French. Contorted our bodies and stretched for huge yellow, blue, and red dots. Found the joey that matched the mother kangaroo. Caught Colonel Mustard with a lead pipe in the ballroom.

And so it was that when I settled into my first tiny apartment as a newly-married, I found a small section of shelf space in the corner of the bathroom for a few well-worn boxes, reinforced with masking tape on the corners. As a young bride, I soon discovered that my amiable, noncompetitive husband rolled dice, flipped cards, and constructed words only to placate my pressing requests. He didn't plan for the kill, didn't wait for the moment of ambush, didn't care, in essence, whether he won the game or not.

Most galling of all, he actually seemed pleased when I won. I realized the futility of pursuing the exercise one Saturday evening when I was engaged in a cutthroat game in the living room with a group of friends. Just as I slapped down the winning stroke, I heard my husband's voice in the kitchen in the midst of a group of more gentle people. "No, you can go first. Really. No, that's quite all right. Go right ahead." While I had plotted and planned, schemed and connived, seized openings, blocked opponents, honed in for the slaughter, he hadn't even started the game yet. It was hopeless.

When my first child came along, I anxiously anticipated the day that I would sit down and play a board game with him. Shortly before he turned five, I realized that I could wait no longer. Coming home one afternoon with a gleaming new version of Candy Land, I sat him down. This, I said, is going to be fun.

He didn't like waiting his turn. He hated drawing a yellow card when the yellow space was only one hop from his present position. He wanted to win. Without the work, without the struggle, he wanted to arrive at the Candy Castle quickly, in short order, and without my plastic playing-piece being anywhere in view of the prize. When I drew the card that advanced me to King Kandy, he fumed in anger. "I hate this game! That's not fair!" But it was the Molasses Swamp that finally finished him off.

"Why do they have a red dot in the middle of the square?" he asked as he plopped his Gingerbread man in the middle of the sticky mass.

"You have to stay there until you draw a red card," I explained.

Two turns later the coveted red block had still not appeared. I never realized how far a deck of cards could sail when thrown by a small fist.

As the months passed, I persisted. Eyeing the toy shelves at department stores, I selected new possibilities. Perhaps, I reasoned on the way home, this will be the one. Every evening after supper and dishes, we settled onto the living room floor. Our joy lasted only as long as his luck held out. Whenever I climbed a ladder and he descended a chute, the torrential rains began. But then one day, in the midst of a game of Sorry, I clacked my green man into his blue one, sending him back to start and covered my head for the reign of terror. Instead, he said with a smile, "You just wait. You're going to be next."

For the next five years, we played Sorry. Sprawled out on the living room floor, we selected cards, circled the board, and marched home. In the back seat of cars, we maneuvered tiny pawns that fit into a square plastic box in the Traveler's version of the game. We played by flashlight in tents, at birthday parties, on long winter evenings.

Other games followed. He learned to wait his turn, pace out his moves, accept defeat graciously. And then his little brother arrived.

Son Number Two, I soon learned, had not been cut out of the same cloth as his brother. While I struggled to get Son Number One to pull a comb through his hair at the age of nine, Son Number Two used up all of my hair spray preening for the perfect image on the first day of kindergarten. When I tried to teach him to play the piano, he pushed my hands away, demanded that I leave, and spent the next hour picking out the melodies playing in his head. Everything I had struggled to understand with my first child, integrated into my understanding of raising children, would be of no avail in this case. A new challenge had begun.

Jeff was introduced to the world of games one rainy afternoon as his older brother and I sat methodically setting up a Monopoly board. "Want to play, Jeff?" asked Eric, interrupting his brother in the midst of a perfect three-minute headstand. He flipped into a smoothly arched recovery, eyed the board with a sweeping gaze, and nodded his assent.

And so the game began. As Eric organized his piles of money, counted his deeds, and planned his slow but steady progress, Jeff cartwheeled around the family room, working toward a precise, symmetrical rotation. He rushed to the board only in response to our caroled "It's your turn," staking his claims, rashly spending money, plotting his big win with reckless certainty.

Forty-five minutes into the game Eric surveyed his holdings. St. Charles Place. New York Avenue. Four railroads. Waterworks. Two five-hundred-dollar bills. Two one-hundreds. Several hundred more in smaller bills. "This is fun," he said, carefully arranging the piles of pastel cash with growing confidence.

Then it was that Jeff landed on Park Place. He mortgaged Marvin Gardens, Indiana Avenue, the Electric Company. He swiftly exchanged every last dollar of his holdings for the blue-bordered deed. He did a frogstand. He waited.

Fifteen minutes later he had Broadway. I knew then that it was only a matter of time.

"I'll take the hotel," he demanded after five more swift circuits of the board. Seizing it from my outstretched hand, he placed it dead-center on the last square before "Go."

Oblivious, Eric arranged his deeds, counted his money, settled back in security. It took him two more turns before he fell into the trap.

"Broadway with one hotel. That'll be $2,000," Jeff demanded.

All color seemed to drain from Eric's face. By some instinct borne of old, I grasped my head and ducked below the potential line of fire. But it was not a scream that shattered my heart but a long, low sigh. He pushed the two five-hundred-dollar bills across the board. He surrendered the hundreds. He counted out the 50s, 20s, 10s, 5s, and 1s. When he was finished, one lone twenty remained on his side of the board.

"It's your turn, Mom," he said.

Mechanically, I advanced my silver car three spaces. Behind me, Jeff executed a perfect handstand. For one long second, time seemed suspended. I sat in the midst of my two children, feeling the tremendous responsibility entrusted to me in the two lives that balanced precariously between hope and despair, dreams and reality.

"It's your turn, Jeff," I finally called.

In the end, it was I who landed on Broadway one too many times. Shut out by my own two sons, I understood at last what it means to experience joy from losing a game. Should I be stripped of all my earthly possessions, my dignity, my station in life, I will be forever grateful if two vulnerable, fragile young lives find themselves in the end with a winning hand. To that end, I continue to play the game of Life, gently easing one fragile heart toward confidence, another toward accepting Pennsylvania Avenue should Broadway be already taken.

Gathering

LIGHT

Dale Slongwhite

"You are the third light," says the Right Reverend M. Thomas Shaw III, and I feel the flame radiate down the darkened aisle, around the post where three candles flicker, through the latched white gate enclosing our small pew, and illuminate my soul. "Carry forth your light in the lantern of yourself," he says, and I vow that I will.

This is the fifth year I have waited in line over an hour outside the Old North Church on the eve of the Massachusetts holiday, Patriot's Day, to commemorate the lighting of the lamps. The church, its tall white spire jutting into the sky, sits on a hill overlooking Boston Harbor, abutted on all sides by colonial-day brick buildings on a narrow cobblestone street designed for horses, not cars. It is here on April 18, 1775, that sexton Robert Newman climbed the narrow steps into the steeple and placed two lighted pewter lanterns in a small window. "One if by land, two if by sea." From across the river in Charlestown, Paul Revere eyed the lanterns and began his famous ride with William Dawes to warn of the march of the British soldiers.

Others took up the cry . . . Dr. Samuel Prescott was leaving his girlfriend's house just after midnight when he ran into Dawes and Revere. He was able to escape when the British surrounded the three of them. He bounded over streams and stone walls to bring the news to Concord. Over the next five days, a twenty-three-year-old farmer, Israel Bissell, galloped 345 miles across five colonies to deliver the message, "A brigade consisting of about 1,000 or 1,200 men marched to Lexington, upon which they fired without any provocation and killed six men and wounded four others...."

On the brick wall in the plaza behind the church, a bronze plaque reads, "To those men of the North End who defended with their lives the hope of their country...." I read the plaque in grateful silence. Because they carried their hope into action, I am free.

Inside, I stand with the congregation and sing lustily. "My country 'tis of thee, Sweet land of liberty, Of thee I sing.... Our fathers' God, to thee, Author of liberty, to Thee we sing: Long may our land be bright, With freedom's holy light; Protect us by Thy might, Great God, our King." The congregation is packed tightly in latched-door, high-back pews on the main floor and three rows in the balcony that encircle the sanctuary. Our voices spiral upward into the vaulted ceiling of the tiny church and around the two massive gold chandeliers hanging from twenty-five-foot cords, around the ancient pipe organ, the three-candle sconces on posts lining the sanctuary, the tall Palladian windows with lilies and tulips on their sills, the speaker's podium on the small enclosed platform ten steps up.

There is pageantry here, ritual, and remembrance. Men with three-cornered black felt hats march in with muskets over their shoulders. They are dressed like militia men in fringed white pants, tan "deerskin" coats belted at the waist, round Ben Franklin glasses. Women in long wool capes and white cotton bonnets follow them. A sixth generation granddaughter of Paul Revere reads Longfellow's poem, "The Midnight Ride of Paul Revere." A sixth generation relative of Robert Newman carries two pewter lanterns into the steeple.

"Freedom is pieced together by millions of acts of courage," Reverend Shaw says. "By people with tiny resources. Let us carry the lantern not only to the tower tonight but take it to our homes, our schools, our work. A few steps, a small candle, illuminate the history of a great nation."

Now the presenters are marching out down the center aisle. The speaker is dressed in a bright red, white, and blue robe and carries a staff taller than himself. In the crook of the staff is a carving of a dove. The organist belts a lively tune through the church. There are drums rat-a-tat-ing, fifes whistling. I open the gate of our pew, on the door is a gold plate—*Daniel Crockford 1724*— and I march down the aisle. I am part of it now. Part of the pageantry. Part of the remembrance. Part of the light.

I am pushed with the throng through the small square lobby and notice bricks encased on the wall that are from a prison in Boston, England, where pilgrims were jailed for their religious beliefs. We spill out into the dark night. People clog the street. A senior-citizen couple lean out the unscreened window of a fifth floor apartment. Others watch from rooftops. There is a cacophony of sound: in the steeple the bell, which was cast by Paul Revere himself, is repeatedly donging; costumed players raise fifes to their lips in synchronization and trill eighteenth century tunes, their fingers rapidly covering and uncovering holes on top of the wooden instruments; beside the fifers, six or seven teenagers roll and tap out the tune on drums suspended by straps from their shoulders; a man with a foot-tall black fur hat firmly strapped about his head and dressed in the red coat of a British soldier fires off a musket, and the crowd jumps in alarm.

I back up the street, the noise dimming to background music, and then I see them—two tiny flickering lights at the base of the steeple. They seem too small to have made such a big difference. I, the third light, also feel too small to make a difference. Yet standing here in the very spot where freedom began, I realize that I am the conduit between the past and the future. It is my duty to pass the torch of my ancestors to future generations. I see myself standing in a long line holding hands with those who have gone before, generation after generation connected together.

There is my mother, who, at twenty-four, agreed to raise her fourteen-year-old brother-in-law when his mother died of a heart attack. There is my grandmother, spunky for her time, insisting she would drive a car. There is my great-grandmother, who gave birth to five babies before one finally lived past a year. On the day her fourteenth child married, the fifteenth child, a young woman dressed as a flapper, rode off on the back of a motorcycle and was killed. But my great-grandmother did not cry. "I have no more tears left," she said. My life is built upon their sacrifices, their vision, their determination, their choices, their tears, their laughter. I am the link between them and my daughters.

I reach forth, grasp the hands of Karen and Laurel, our fingers intertwine. I squeeze, infusing all I have—the beliefs, the values, the hopes, the dreams of myself and those who have gone before. They take what I offer, guard it, fan it, expand upon it. And with their other hand, they stretch off camera, to someone we cannot yet see who will carry forth our heritage. Perhaps it will be a Robert Newman who gives the secret signal. Or a Paul Revere, who is the first to start the journey. Or a Samuel Prescott, who bounds ahead when the others are captured. Or a farmer Israel Bissell, who brings the light the farthest.

Meditatively, I turn and begin the long walk to our car. Behind me the bells are still pealing, the fifes are still trilling, the drums are still tapping out a tune. The sounds begin to fade in the distance. Within me, I carry the light of one lantern. I am one small act of courage. I am the history of the future and will guard that charge with my life.

Gathering

THE UNEXPECTED

Sandra Doran

I never expected to stand in front of the Old South Church in Boston, Massachusetts, in flowing black and red regalia, hands at my sides, as two robed professors garnished my neck with a silken-lined hood. I didn't start out my life planning to earn a doctoral degree. Didn't envision the march with black velvet tam, golden tassel, strains of Bach vibrating each step down the mahogany aisle toward completion. I never dreamed I would derive such joy out of the little band of supporters clustered in the first row, cameras flashing, grins exuding the essence of their own delight.

Looking at the framed Boston University diploma hanging on my study wall, I am humbled and awed, still, at the memories of the circumstances and miracles that enabled me to take the journey of faith that led me to a time and place previously unimagined.

Securing a teaching job on a college campus recently, I took part in a tour, familiarizing new faculty with the surroundings that would provide the resources and environment to support our roles. "And this is our library," the young woman announced, swinging open the glass doors and ushering our small group into the hushed, well-stocked first floor. "We call this the pit," she indicated, pointing out a sunken area with maroon couches, magazine-strewn tables, and softly lighted lamps.

The scene looked vaguely reminiscent, and I tuned out the remainder of her speech, trying to recall when I had been in the spot before. As if in the midst of a deja-vu, I felt my eyes sweeping the couches, the tables, and the shelves behind them for some clue. And then my gaze stopped. Two shelves of thick blue volumes arrested my search. I wandered from the group, selected a book from its place, and sat on the couch, remembering.

Five years evaporated in haste as I recalled how the notion had come into my head one evening, as unexpectedly as a rain shower on a cloudless morning. "Maybe I'll go for a doctorate," I had stated, feeling foolish even as the words found their way into being. But how does one take the first step toward something so illusive, so unanticipated, so uncharted in one's family?

I remembered ferreting through a drawer for some paper, scratching out names of colleges, dragging out the worn atlas from the car, examining it for possibilities. The details paraded themselves before my consciousness as I replaced the book on the library shelf, rejoined the tour. I had called a college in a nearby city the next afternoon, I remembered, asking whether they had listings of degrees offered at other universities. Following the librarian's directions I found the school, located the library, and inquired as to the placement of the books detailing the offerings of universities in North America. She had pointed me toward a group of thick, blue volumes, shelved behind a sunken area, furnished with maroon couches, magazine-strewn tables, softly lighted lamps. This place, I realized, with a surprising lump in my throat. Five years ago.

Reaching out on a whim. Knowing nothing of research methods, the subway system winding underneath the city of Boston, comprehensive examinations, first hearings. Never dreaming I would return to this spot, degree behind me, classes of students before me.

I walked with the group, drifting forward, caught now in the arms of memories that enfolded me in a broad circle, arching the past forward to this place and time.

I remembered the commute, the endless hours planning and mapping out the journey, the first drive to the city, threading my way through five lanes of traffic, driving through branching tunnels, my father's words echoing in my ears, "Stay in your own lane," as exits passed and walls of metal and wheels closed me in.

I remembered finding my way off, out, into deeper mazes, heart pounding as carefully written directions found no connection to honking horns, one-way streets, the insistent staccato of jackhammers, Chinese takeouts, record shops, sidewalks thronged by men in suits, a student pushing a cello case, young mothers gripping the hands of children, a woman with blue hair that spiked upward in exclamation points aimed at the sky. I remembered arriving somehow, that first afternoon, sitting in class knowing that the ride back loomed inevitable, emerging from the building in darkness, searching in vain for the roads that would take me home.

I remembered entering the city by train the next week, hoping that public transportation would offer a better option, leaving class in quick, watchful steps, waiting for the "T." I remembered standing wedged in the midst of the old and the young, gripping a metal bar as the green creaking machine carried me to the train station, murmuring apologies as I lurched into the side of a garlic-drenched passenger beside me, his stone face signaling my greater error of breaking the apathetic code of the city. I recalled being dumped once again into the chilly night air, walking five blocks to the train station, sitting on cold, gray stone, weary of body and mind, warily gripping a briefcase beside me. I remembered aching for the board on the wall to announce the 10:00 p.m. rush of wind that would take me to the green freshness of the suburbs, the sweet night air of home, the three people whose lives seemed all the more vibrant and real, measured against the backdrop of train whistles and faceless travelers.

Walking with my campus tour group past students hard at work in the study carrels, I remembered my own five labor-intensive years devoted to the acquisition of knowledge and the pinching of pennies that made it possible. I recalled fighting the City of Boston over the price of a traffic ticket and winning, discovering that a bagel is the cheapest way to quiet a grumbling stomach, shrinking down articles in the library on the copy machine to fit more than one page on the screen at a time, accepting speaking appointments to distant places to finance coursework, writing papers on planes, collapsing on benches in airport terminals with highlighters sweeping across lines of print on photocopied pieces of research.

Eyeing the students hunched over their books, I recalled my struggles grasping the code of scholarly language; papers filling the floor of my study; diagrams attempted, balled up, thrown away. One scene seemed so unplausible, so strikingly out of place that it appeared surreal, like something I had viewed long ago on black-and-white television. I remembered accepting a speaking appointment in Florida, being given a day-long pass to "Wet and Wild," alternating my day between careening down thunderous rivers and sitting straight in a lounge chair, determinedly reviewing data while vacationers ran by oblivious, yellow tubes dripping water on the pages of my open books and papers, research materials spread out in piles on tables and chairs.

I recalled the saga of my research project that led me to step onto a decaying porch that threatened to send my foot through the rotting steps; to ring the bell of a half-million-dollar home flanked by tennis courts, swimming pool, and manicured expanses of lawn; to talk to strangers who through the telling of their stories became known and understood. I recalled the frenetic rush to completion; the notes pasted to my walls; the charts; the torn pieces of paper with scrawled ideas; the emergence from my study, 456 pages later with the weak, triumphant pronouncement, "It's done," while my nine-year-old son asked in innocence and incredulity, "You finished it? Your declaration of independence?"

The tour wound its way back to the parking lot and prepared to leave the campus. But one more memory remained. The glorious day that put it all into perspective; that melted the memory of the coldness of stone under my legs in a late-night train station; that erased the tension of balled-up paper, aborted ideas, empty wallets, the pull of a briefcase strap on a sore shoulder.

We marched back down the aisle of the Old South Church, a bevy of red-robed scholars newly hooded. The ceremony over, we anticipated reunions with family, waiting friends. But all was not yet over. Exiting the sanctuary, I unexpectedly found myself in a long, narrow foyer. Lining the walls on either side stood the faculty, the colors of their robes forming a vision of pomp, magnificence. And then I heard it. Softly at first and then louder, crescendoing, clamorous. They were applauding. These professors who had challenged me, questioned me, sent me back to "Go" more times than I could remember, awed me, inspired me, intimidated me, loomed above me on planes that eluded even my highest thoughts. They were applauding. For me.

Something in my throat caught then; a bird flapped its feathered wings in a flurried moment of pride and humility, awe, and amazement. I lifted my head and caught the gaze of my equals. I had never expected such a moment.

Gathering

POSSIBILITIES

Dale Slongwhite

Excerpt from admissions essay to Harvard University Extension School, by Karen Slongwhite Mikhail:

> *"Early in my grandmother's high school career, one of her teachers recognized that she had potential and encouraged her to take college prep courses. She did very well, but the family did not have the money for further education. So the day after graduation, my grandmother put her dreams of college behind her and began walking every day to her job in the factory with her father.*
>
> *"My parents met and began dating when they were sixteen years old. By the time they graduated from high school two years later, they knew they would be married; therefore, my mother decided to take a two-year secretarial degree. After graduation, she got married and went to work full time while my father finished his bachelor's degree. But my mom always wanted a four-year degree. Over the years, she took a course here and a course there—anything that would fit into her schedule and that she found interesting. It took twenty-five years and eight colleges, but she finally got a bachelor's*

in communications.

"Both of these stories are part of my history and part of what makes an education important to me. Getting an education is not necessarily about getting a new job, although that is one of the goals I have. It is about pursuing the things that are interesting to me, knowing more about the world, and personal growth. I believe that an education should expand your horizons and cause you to look at the world in a new and exciting way. An education is a personal achievement.

"I have not taken a straight path in my college career so far. I also chose to get married before I finished my degree, and I am now balancing a marriage, a full-time job, and twelve hours of credits. Harvard is my third college, and I am already older than a traditional student who goes straight from high school through four years of college. However, I have always moved forward, and I will obtain my degree.

"Someday my daughter will understand the importance of a higher education by hearing the stories of her mother, grandmother, and great-grandmother."

"I think I want to be a medical librarian," Karen said with enthusiasm. "I read about it in a book called *Careers for Bookworms and Other Literary Types.*"

We both laughed. She reads by flashlight. She reads during lunch. She reads on the train. She reads on vacation. She reads children's books in Spanish. She taught herself to read in the car by keeping the window open and sticking her head out to gulp fresh air when she felt sick. She read *A Tale of Two Cities* thirteen times because she did not like it the first five times through but felt she was missing something. Yes, she had found an appropriate book.

At twenty-four, Karen had taken the day off from work to explore Harvard's career library, hoping to find a clue to her future. She was majoring in biology, a second semester junior, but unsure of what she would do upon graduation. Last year she wanted to be an economist. Before that, an elementary school-teacher. Before that, an environmentalist. I can see her in any one of these careers.

"I loved researching my paper last semester in the Countway Medical Library," she said. "I think being a medical librarian would tie together my biology major and my love of books. I mean, I can find things in the library that librarians can't. Ask Laurel!"

In her *Current Topics in Medicine* class last semester, she used the library affiliated with Harvard Medical School to search medical journals for her paper on removing children from antiepileptic medications after they've been seizure free for a year. To Karen, it was not just a writing assignment to fulfill an academic requirement—it was a quest into her own history. She quizzed me on the details of the seizures she experienced from the age of ten months to six years, and she contacted the pediatric neurologist who made the decision to remove her from Tegretol when she was seven. When I drove her to the class in the heart of Cambridge, I studied my studious daughter. Beyond the married woman, beyond the Harvard student, not too far beyond, I could see the infant, limp as a rag doll in my arms, eyes rolled back into her sweaty colorless face, softly grunting. Where have the years gone between then and now?

To Karen, the world is a place of hope, full of possibilities too numerous to harness. Narrowing it down to just one thing, which to her means eliminating so much, has proven to be a difficult task. She has read countless books on gardening and home-schooling and can picture herself as a stay-at-home mom living in the country, teaching her as-yet-unconceived children at home, canning her own vegetables. By the same token, she is energized by the culture, entertainment, education, history, and opportunities of Boston and can imagine living in it or near it for the rest of her life. But to do either is to eliminate the other, and she is not ready to limit her possibilities.

During the two summers Karen researched gardening, our family rented a 20 feet by 40 feet plot in a nearby community garden and raised beefsteak and cherry tomatoes, peppers, zucchini, lettuce, and corn. From her reading, she taught us to plant marigolds beside tomatoes in order to control pests and to rotate our crops the second year to use different nutrients from the soil. For three years during the time period she wanted to be an environmentalist, I accompanied her to the largest environmental conference in the world, at Tuft's University, because she was too young to drive. We heard speakers such as Bruce E. Babbitt, secretary of the United States Department of the Interior, and Dr. Nehemiah arap Rotich, executive director of the East Africa Wildlife Society. We attended workshops on writing for the environment, protecting drinking water, sustainable living. Beside her, and because of her, I learned.

Transition points are difficult for me. I tend to look at what I have lost, not at what I have gained. Things I took for granted that are now gone suddenly seem extremely valuable to me. Karen, on the other hand, has developed a way of looking at losses as temporary and change as loaded with possibilities. She recently moved from a four-room apartment to one room. She's thrilled to have a door directly to the outside with a patch of grass for white resin chairs and a table and to have room for planters of herbs, vegetables, and flowers. Less to clean, she says, she can walk to work, it's much quieter off the main street, and they can save money.

To Karen, problems are pests to be swatted, annoyances to be pushed aside. When she was in the seventh grade, she sneaked into Boston on the subway with a friend. We had just moved to the area, but she had no problem reading signs and navigating around a city she'd never seen. When the train whizzed past their destination without stopping, the friend panicked. "What'll we do?"

"We have two choices," Karen said, unfazed. "We can get off at the next stop and get on the train heading back. Maybe that will stop at North Station. Or," she pointed to the map on the wall of the subway car, "we can get off at Haymarket and change to the green line."

When Karen dropped out of college at nineteen, David and I feared she would never complete her education. We tried to talk her into staying in school, living in the dorm, developing friendships, participating in the social aspect of college. As it turned out, she prefers classes in the evening with adults serious about the coursework. An apartment is more appealing to her than a dorm, a husband more meaningful than school functions.

Karen landed her first job on her fourteenth birthday. She found out that the hospital where David worked hired students at fourteen. Without telling us, she walked into Human Resources on her birthday and filled out an application. After school for the next seven months, she changed into blue scrubs, entered the sterile processing department, and delinted operating room towels with an adhesive roller. She saved most of the money she earned, and the next year when we sent her to live with her uncle's family and attend school at the Stanborough Park School in Watford, Hertfordshire, England, she took a trip with them through Germany, Belgium, and the Netherlands.

Shortly after her fifteenth birthday, she wrote a letter home from England. "Either I'm gettin' old or I'm having fun," she said. "Time seems to flow through my hands like grains of sand, and I don't know where it is going. It has been nearly three months since I was home for Christmas, and it seems like yesterday. I have only another three months until I get home to stay for another three years. Yes, it *is* only another three years. After that I'll go away to college, and then I'll get married, and you'll almost never see me. It seems ridiculous!"

It seems ridiculous to me that almost all of it has come true—everything except the "almost never see me" part. We talk every day and get together at least once a week.

Maybe Karen *will* be a medical librarian. Maybe she will be something else. Who knows? Her world is filled with possibilities . . . possibilities she has taught me to see.

Gathering

AWARENESS

Sandra Doran

I first began to realize that I was no longer young when I was hit in the rear by a 1995 Pontiac. Relating the story to family and friends, I said, "And then some kid backed out of his driveway and hit me." The "kid," I found out later, was twenty-five years old.

About the same time, I began to notice that everybody I once thought of as sage and wise and significantly older than myself looked like a kid. Driving down the road, I'd see an officer at a construction site. A kid with a police hat on. Checking in at a new doctor's office, I'd look up from my magazine to catch a glimpse of the physician beckoning me forward. A girl with a stethoscope around her neck. Hardest of all was boarding a plane. Suddenly I'd realize that I was putting my life in the hands of a kid wearing a pilot's uniform.

All of this, I am discovering, has something to do with this whole thing they call midlife crisis. Suddenly you realize that it's not just a matter of age that is keeping you from being the anchor on "Good Morning America." There's not some magical moment when you're going to arrive. Fact is, you're probably as good as you're going to get.

I say this not with the resigned sigh of a disillusioned cynic but with the sincere effort of an optimist stretching toward realism. There are times in our lives, I have found, when we simply have to look at the facts, cut our losses, and readjust our inner vision. When life deals you one of those moments, you know.

I was sifting through some mail in my office last fall when I came across an announcement from the Health Services Department. There would be a free health screening for faculty members, the notice said. The spot on my leg looked like nothing, but there was no harm in being sure. I dialed the campus extension and secured an appointment.

"It could be nothing," the doctor told me. "But just to be sure . . ." he handed me a business card. Probably nothing, I told myself. But there was no harm in being sure.

Biopsy completed, I dismissed the thought from my mind. Ten days later a scrawled note in my datebook prompted me to call the office. "Mrs. Doran?" came the voice on the other end. "Let me get the doctor."

I gripped the phone a bit tighter, my heart beginning to race. "Mrs. Doran? The good news is that you have the most mild form of cancer. It's called basal-cell or squamous carcinoma, which we've caught in the early stages . . ."

It wasn't the cancer itself that sent my inner world spinning. Not the procedure I'd have to face. Not the needles going into my leg, not the "scoop and burn" in the doctor's office, not even the penny-shaped faded purple scar appearing four inches below my knee. It was what it all stood for. What it all meant. The loss of carefree summer days. The inability to ever again sit in a beach chair and feel the troubles of life washing away with the tides. Like the Nathaniel Hawthorne character whose life would be forever marked by the knowledge of evil, I would face life, after that one phone call, with a knowledge that had the power to inhibit joy and stymie freedom. Sun-screen and beach umbrellas and wide floppy hats notwithstanding, I would feel the sand under my toes, the surf on my face, the sun on my back with a tinge of fear from this moment on.

Such a sentence can only be understood in the context of my love affair with the beach, which dates back to my earliest memories and weaves its way through all the phases of my life. I learned early to associate joy with seagulls and low tide, dried beach grass and chipped clam shells, icy cold swims and salt on my tongue. As a child, I sat on the beach and popped handfuls of dripping green rockweed, lined up periwinkles for races, stirred driftwood in make-believe rock stoves. As a teenager, I grabbed towel and radio, tanning lotion and sandwich, and headed for the one place I could lie down and think without feeling as if I ought to be catching up on homework, sewing a dress, studying for my SATs. As a young mother, I escaped tension and toy-cluttered rooms by loading the car with plastic boats, juice boxes, crib-in-a-tent. While the baby slept and my active toddler dug tunnels to China, I sat high on the dunes, thinking, writing, breathing in the glory of blue sky and golden sands, knowing that all was right with the world.

As the children grew, the beach still beckoned with its no-lose offer. Free entertainment. Spectacular views. Something for everyone. Relaxation and exercise. Rejuvenation of the spirit. Last summer I took to loading up the car with my two sons and their friends, boogie boards, snorkels, buckets, goggles. Late afternoon we'd return, buckets filled with shells, seaweed trailing our feet, sand filling the car by degrees.

And this summer? I sit at my desk in February, wondering what it will be like. "Why did Adam and Eve have to eat that stupid apple?" my young son once asked, leaving me answerless and stumbling. Whatever the motivation of our first parents, we are left on this planet with the knowledge of good and evil. A knowledge that reminds us that no matter how bright the sun, invigorating the waves, mild the breeze, we are but vulnerable travelers in temporary houses on a crumbling planet. At such times, it is only our faith that gives strength for the journey.

Gathering

THE BOUNTY

Dale Slongwhite

I wonder how many times I have entered a grocery store, chosen a wire cart, checked its wheels for squeaking or sticking, and embarked on the adventure of gathering the bounty for my family. I wonder how many times I have chosen what they would draw from a cooler at the beach, nibble on as we played games on Saturday night, or stab with a fork when they talked about their day. In twenty-seven years of marriage, I can't even begin to estimate.

The first time, as a young bride of twenty in South Lancaster, Massachusetts, I didn't bring enough money. I felt proud and grown-up wheeling the cart up and down the aisles, dropping in spices and flour and bread and orange juice to stock my very own refrigerator and cupboards. When the tally was announced and I was $5 short, I had to leave the paper-bagged groceries and race home two miles for more money. I was so embarrassed I never returned to that store in the two years we lived there.

Back then, I shopped predictably every Thursday evening after supper, keeping track of the total with a three-buttoned red clicker. If I spent less than the $20 in my purse, I'd use the remainder on something personal for me. Every few months I'd splurge and buy four frozen Morton Honey Buns for thirty-nine cents. We'd heat them in the oven and savor each sugar-drizzled morsel. We lived in married-student housing at the college, and the husbands would meet at the dumpster scraping out casseroles and swapping warnings. "Do you have the Betty Crocker cookbook?" they'd ask. "Don't try the recipe on page forty-two." The apartment was on the road to the college farm, and we bought our milk there for $1 a gallon, walking home carrying the returnable glass bottle by its heavy-duty plastic handle.

When David graduated and we moved to Tennessee for his first teaching job, I shopped in Kroger, where "grits" was listed on the aisle marker. "What's grits?" I questioned, until Karen was born and the hospital served the cornmeal-like substance as a side dish to every meal. Although it's much harder to find since I've returned to New England, I always keep a small cylindrical box of grits beside the Cheerios on my cereal shelf.

In Tennessee when I did not work, we switched to powdered milk to save money and rarely bought Honey Buns. We ate our dinner watching *McHale's Navy* reruns on my Aunt Lucy's old black-and-white portable set until Karen was born. Then I insisted the TV be turned off during mealtime. I wanted dinner to be like it was in my home of origin. There, dinner was my mother's daily offering to the family. Her day revolved around it. In the morning she planned the menu and removed ingredients from her freezer. In the early afternoon she cooked potatoes and casseroles and dessert from scratch. In the late afternoon she shredded lettuce and chopped tomatoes and diced carrots for salads. At 5:00—on the dot—my mother, father, brother, two sisters, and I gathered around the steel-legged gray Formica table to discuss our day. We left home each morning, it seemed, only to have tales to regale the others at dinner.

When my own children were babies, I left the home twice a week—once to attend church, once to buy groceries. At 8:00 p.m. on Thursday evening when I was sure everything was under control on the homefront, I drove to the store and for one hour entered the world of other adults. Slowly I wheeled the carriage up and down the aisles, comparing labels for nutritive and budgetary value. I chose mixed vegetables so I could put them on the tray of the highchair with the instructions, "Eat the square orange ones. Now see if you can find the round green ones." I chose crackers and bananas—food that didn't require dexterity with utensils. At lunchtime I held books in front of the highchairs and read upside down while the girls fed themselves.

By the time I took a job working four evenings a week, our dinner hour had been firmly ensconced as sacred time. David did not linger at the end of his teaching day and arrived home for dinner at 3:45. When I left for work at 4:15, it was he who cleaned up the kitchen.

Over the years I have cut thousands of coupons, exchanging them with friends and organizing them in carefully-labeled sections of a small box. I have stood in front of cans and boxes with a calculator and figured the best buy—or brought Karen, who could do the calculations in her head while keeping track within pennies of the mounting bill. I have bought food for lunch boxes, food for picnics, food for church potlucks, food for birthday parties, food for guests, food for holidays, food for nutritional value, food for treats. I have blended, boiled, baked, steamed, microwaved, frozen, and gelled. I have cut recipes out of newspapers and magazines, checked cookbooks out of the library, purchased numerous specialty cookbooks, and produced a cookbook of favorite family recipes, complete with photos of family members eating.

For several months after Karen married, I drove twenty-five miles every other week to shop with her. The event took all evening as we meandered down aisles and exchanged coupons, ideas, recipes, stories, and plans.

Shopping has taken on a new form now that the girls are grown and have left home. I buy skim milk for me and lactaid for

David. I buy plum tomatoes because they are smaller and just right for a salad for two. I buy low-calorie, high-fiber bread to accommodate our Weight Watchers diet. I buy more bananas because I eat one for breakfast every morning in the car as I drive to work. I buy things once considered too extravagant for earlier budgets: peeled baby carrots, flavored sparkling water, frozen blueberries. I've discovered I like yogurt after all.

Our busy life no longer allows for a set "time" or "budget" or "coupon clipping." With just David and me home, we dash in and out of random grocery stores "for just a few items" after Weight Watchers or water aerobics classes. He wheels the basket and packs each item so carefully you'd think the cart was going to be moved across America. My purchases have never had it so good. I cook only three meals a week these days—on weekends. The rest of the time we eat lunch in our company cafeterias and leftovers or sandwiches for supper.

Sometimes it seems that my adult life has revolved around food—buying it, carrying it out of the grocery store and into my home, stacking it in the cupboard or fridge, planning meals, cooking it, eating it, washing the dishes afterward. I wonder what my life would be like if dietitians were to create a pill to take the place of food. What would I do with all my spare time?

On the other hand, food is more than physical nourishment. It is what reminds me three times a day to bow my head in thankfulness to my heavenly Father. It serves as mile-markers of where we are and have been in life. It is the medium that has drawn me together with those I love. When else except around a table laden with food would I sit so close for so long to a son-in-law or a nephew or an aunt? When else would I stand with far-away relatives, hold hands with them, and sing "There is so much for which to be thankful"? I don't know if I ever would have heard about my children's days or their well-formed opinions on world events or local crises if a plate of spaghetti had not been before them.

With lasagna and chocolate cake, we have celebrated birthdays; with sparkling grape juice, we have toasted each other on New Year's Eve; with eight bushels of apples and a canner, we have talked and laughed in the kitchen every Columbus Day as we preserve over one hundred quarts of applesauce; in the garden, we have sweated and planned for the future together; on holidays, we have prepared traditions of green bean "ensemble," cranberry-raspberry jello and mashed carrots and turnips.

Gathering the bounty has taken a lot of my time over the years, but in my opinion, it has been time well-spent.

Gathering

A FAMILY

Sandra Doran

We huddled together beneath the bowels of the earth, beyond cold, beyond numb, beyond exhausted. Ten-year-old Jeffrey stared ahead at the tracks, willing the train to pull into the station. Eric, Jr. leaned his thirteen years against my shoulder, unable to hold his head up any longer. His father stamped his feet and checked the arrival board against his watch. Suddenly a scratchy sound announced the activation of the loudspeaker system. "May I have your attention please? May I have your attention? The midnight train to Attleboro has been canceled. The next arrival will be at 1:00 a.m."

We stared at one another in disbelief, the festivities of the day fading into the reality of one more hour in sub-zero temperatures in Boston in the middle of the night. Slowly we gathered our belongings. Pulled on backpacks. Lifted our tired bodies from concrete benches.

Somehow we managed to stumble back up the stairs, out into the street. Somewhere fireworks were shooting off. A band played "Auld Lang Syne." Cries of "Happy New Year!" filled the air. Moving one wooden foot in front of the other, we advanced, a horizontal line, arms linked, toward a doughnut shop across four wide lanes of traffic. Inside, we ordered hot chocolate, cinnamon buns. It was Jeffrey who spoke first. "First night," he said crypti-cally, "has just become Worst night." He smiled then, a wry smile that took all of us off guard, melted our frozen faces into laughter, sent us sputtering into our drinks.

And when I think back on our New Year's Eve celebration of 1996, I am gripped not by my remembrance of the cold but of the warmth. We waited out the hour. We boarded the train. We told silly jokes. We staggered into our beds at 2:30 a.m. We praised the Lord for woolen blankets and electric heat. We wafted our "Good nights" from room to room. We slept with undisturbed dreams of family and popcorn and hands enfolded together through layers of gloves and mittens.

We are a family, we four, with no thanks to biology, no con-nection by blood, no genes to mark us as having emanated from similar stock. We are a family by choice, a quartet of differences, a foursome of love.

When I tell people that I was swimming laps in a pool while my first son was being born, I always get a few raised eyebrows. We had placed our name on an adoption list one and a half years earlier, having decided that the manner in which our family might come to us was less important than the bonds we would build once children arrived. We would have a daughter, we decided, filling the spare room with dresses passed down from Dale's girls.

"But what if the agency calls and tells you they have a boy waiting?" asked an infinitely wiser man, the father of an adoptive son himself. "We have a choice in the matter," we replied. "We are putting in for girls."

But when we went to decorate the room, we found a com-fortable rust-colored rocker on sale. And pink would certainly not go with rust. Blue would.

"She will be a tomboy," we told those who peeked into the last room down the hall on the right, taking in the blue wallpaper, quilt, bumper-pads. Looking back, I can almost see Someone smiling.

I spent my thirtieth birthday at an infertility clinic, not knowing that my son was nine months in utero. The news came three weeks later, just as we were about to stop looking in the room down the hall, just as the dark days of late winter began to consume us with oppression.

"We are going out to eat," Eric announced as I entered the house after my late morning swim at the YMCA.

"You forgot to put the potatoes in," I stated.

"No," he countered. "The agency called." And then, as my heart lurched, "But Sandy, don't get your hopes up. It's a boy."

We were oddly quiet in the car, our hearts and minds racing in a thousand directions. We ordered pizza at a small family restaurant, populated that Wednesday morning by children of only one gender. A small boy toddled past our table in pursuit of a ball. An infant in soft-blue wool snuggled contentedly into his mother's arms at the next booth. Two preschool boys giggled over a private joke behind us. A young lad grasped his grandpa's hand on their way to the register. Around us, behind us, before us, boys laughed and played and connected with family. Not a single female child entered the restaurant.

That evening, still pondering our decision, we joined our congregation for prayer meeting. "Any silent prayer requests?" asked a member at the close of the service. Yes, we nodded. We had a prayer request. A big one.

"Would you mind giving me a ride home?" asked a member who had never asked before and never would again, whose home was situated far out in the country, nestled into the hills of the Adirondacks. As we drove through miles of countryside on our return trip, our thoughts flowed. We talked of family while the road twisted and turned at unforeseen angles, carrying us in directions that we could not anticipate from one curve to the next.

We reviewed the facts from the torn-off sheet of paper, scribbled in haste in the midst of what had been an ordinary morning. "Boy. Two days old. Physically perfect. Normal delivery. Normal hospital stay. Six pounds, seven ounces."

But it wasn't the facts of the case that drew us toward our son, the well-educated family in his background, the "good genes" described by the adoption agency. It was something deeper, something struggling to take shape, a voice that could not be silenced, a knowledge that our destiny was unraveling before our eyes.

"I'm so glad you called," the secretary on the West Coast answered as we both gripped a telephone extension in our hands. "I'd like to know how to spell his name for the birth certificate."

I dropped into a chair in the living room. Eric paced the floor in the kitchen.

"We'll fly him down to you on Friday . . ."

"As in two days from now?" I questioned, my mouth suddenly dry.

"We can't do that," Eric added. "We have a parenting seminar going on this weekend at our church. We've been planning it for months now. Friday night we'll be having . . . "

"What better way to kick it off," came the response, "than by becoming parents yourselves?"

On Thursday we bought one blue sleeper, one blue hat, one package of diapers, a dozen bottles, and a diaper bag. We ate butterscotch brownies for supper. We stayed up until 2:00 a.m. playing *Trivial Pursuit,* not listening to the questions, not knowing the answers.

On Friday we packed the diaper bag, feeling strangely out of place as we carried it to the car, like children playing house with an empty baby carriage. At the airport we waited with stern faces, each consumed by our own fears. *What if I don't love him?* I struggled to push the thought aside. *What if I look into his face and he looks like someone else's baby, not my own? What if he resembles no one that I have ever loved, his unfamiliarity too great for me to bear?*

The photos in the fourteen-year-old album bear testimony to our thoughts. Waiting for the plane, we are fearful, solemn, grave.

The announcement of the flight's arrival summoned a flurry of people to the bottom of the ramp. We waited, a childless couple in the midst of a giant blur of family reunions, colors, and voices reverberating around us as if in a dream. Scanning the line of travelers we saw no one we knew, no child, no son who would become our own. The pilot exited the plane. The stewardesses dragged their black bags down the ramp.

I twisted the strap of the diaper bag in my hands, turned, and looked away. When I finally turned back for one last check, a woman was making her way down the empty ramp, a bundle of blankets carried gently in her arms. Eric spied out a bank of empty chairs, shepherded the carrier of our son to a quiet corner in the midst of the clamor where the three of us sat down. She placed him on my lap then, and I began to unwrap blankets, my heart thudding. When he was finally unwrapped, I beheld every baby born to my family, every niece I had ever peered at through the glass of a maternity window, my nephew, my husband, myself. My son.

The pictures in the fourteen-year-old album change sharply once this boy has entered our lives. We are no longer grave. We are no longer solemn. My husband's face radiates a smile that lights up the whole terminal. I wipe at tears that refuse to subside. We are a threesome. A family, not connected by chromosomes, not joined by genes, but by a bond that exceeds mere biology.

And that is only half the story.

The second call came three and a half years later.

We had strapped Eric, Jr. into his car seat in the driveway of my parents' home, wishing that the Christmas holiday had not come to an end, that we did not have to face the decision to disconnect life support for my husband's father, when my mother opened the back door.

"Eric," she called out. "Long-distance phone call for you."

My sisters and their families stopped packing their cars. We all filed solemnly back into the living room, seating ourselves on the couch. "It must be his father," I whispered, and they all nodded. "He's gone."

But as the silence thickened, I heard a single word float into the living room from where Eric stood in the kitchen, telephone in his hands. "Fern."

I had only met one Fern in my life. She delivered a five-day-old boy to my arms in a crowded airport in Albany, New York, forever changing my name to "Mom."

"Fern?" We exchanged amazed glances in the living room. Took one long, collective breath. Strained for the details.

"Boy," we heard him say. "Six pounds. Twelve ounces."

"I expected it to be a call of death," said Eric when he finally replaced the receiver. "It was a call of life."

We mailed all of the small dresses back to Dale when we arrived home that night. Our second son would not be needing them.

The day Jeffrey was scheduled to arrive, a storm blew into the New England coast, clogging highways, stranding motorists, and closing airports. "We're stuck somewhere in the Midwest," came the call from Fern. "I'll call you if we can get another flight out."

The three of us circled the living room, pacing, thinking, marking the piling of drifts outside our windows. An hour passed before the phone rang again.

"Can you drive out to New Jersey?" Fern asked. "They're accepting incoming flights."

She had barely finished the question before we piled into our small Chevette, wolfing down sandwiches and weaving down slick roads at top speed.

"The flight's twenty minutes late," Eric announced in relief as we ran into the Newark terminal. "He hasn't arrived yet."

We positioned ourselves before the window, anxious now, experienced.

He was dressed in a borrowed snowsuit, his tiny face submerged in layers of blue. I waited as Eric, Jr. seated himself and stretched out his arms for his brother.

The album shows him grinning, the first to hold the new addition. His father and I are standing proudly behind. Gathering a family.

Gathering

WARMTH

Dale Slongwhite

"Follow me!" she called over her shoulder in the first English we'd heard all morning, and even though we did not know this stranger in a strange land, we clutched the totebags holding our bathing suits and binoculars, loped the length of the dock, jumped into her Land Rover, and held on as she pulled out into the main drag of Cancun. We'd only met her three minutes before, and we didn't know where we were going or why, but we trusted that she would fill us in on the details. "When I pull into the parking lot, open your doors and start running," she said. "I've radioed ahead. They're pulling over the boat for you to jump in."

Six weeks after Laurel left home at the age of twenty-two to complete her education living in the dorm, David and I celebrated with a week-long vacation to the Caribbean. Now don't read more into that than is intended. I just mean that I believe in marking moments, celebrating rites of passage, and that certainly *was* one. Our last child was leaving home, and our relationship was intact.

Deftly, she darted in and out of traffic then pulled into a parking lot. To our right, we spotted the two-decker boat just now inching under the bridge spanning the canal and to our left glittered the expansive sea. We flung open the car doors and took off running, calling Thank yous to a woman who cared enough to save the day for two tourists. On the boat, they caught sight of us and slowed the engines, the sea bubbling and churning great swells at the stern. When it was still two feet from the dock, someone called "Jump!" so we did, hands and knees trembling.

A man in khaki shorts, shirt, and floppy hat thrust a clear plastic cup of diced fresh fruit into one of my hands and a cup of fresh-squeezed orange juice into the other. "Thank you," I said with ashen lips, looking around and realizing that our unorthodox arrival thirty minutes after embarkment now held the attention of the rest of the passengers.

David looked down and patted my hand. "We made it," he said, and I nodded, forcing myself to breathe deeply, feeling the beat of my heart begin to slow, relaxation borne by the tropical sun and sea begin to flow through my veins.

Exotic vacations have never been our norm. Over the years, we've done things like live with Sandra's family for a week in upstate New York or rent a ramshackle cabin on a lake in New Hampshire. But due to the symbolism of the occasion, this trip had to be different. We were celebrating a marriage that had made it through parenting and intended to make it beyond; therefore, we had to do something that would cause those who knew us to ask in shock, "You went *where*?" Something we could look back on with slit-eyed gloating as though we had sneaked in something we shouldn't have. So we booked ourselves into a five-star resort on the Yucatan Peninsula of Mexico.

Some days we relaxed at the resort with its maze of molded-brick sidewalks winding through magnificently appointed grounds of exotic yellow, purple, and red flowers; its beach of glistening white sand that didn't burn our feet; its salty turquoise water the perfect temperature. We chose lounge chairs near palm trees and moved them with the shade to keep our pale New England skin from scorching. One morning we paddled out a great distance in a plastic kayak to photograph the resort with a waterproof camera. Throughout the day, we nibbled on snacks and sipped drinks from either of the open-air cabanas at the edge of the beach—fruit drinks with names like *Merengue, Cococabana, Green Peace*. And we gathered the warmth.

For dinner, we dressed. Waiters pulled out our chairs in the plush dining room, removed china as the last morsel was finished. We walked up and down the seventy-foot aisle lined with food stations, choosing delectable gourmet food beautifully presented among papayas carved like swans; salads encircled with thin slices of cantaloupe, tomato, and oranges; and frilled cucumber flowers set in a carved watermelon vase. We drank juice blended to order—banana, cantaloupe, papaya, pineapple, orange.

In the evening, we walked the darkened beach and watched the lights wink on at the island of Cozumel. We listened to calypso music at the "Margarita." We relaxed in the lobby, soaking in the ambiance—in the center of the open-air tiled lobby, an enormous bouquet of ceramic calla lilies graced a glass-topped table. Above the calla lilies hung a huge four-tiered chandelier from a domed ceiling mottled blue and white to look like sky and clouds. To the right sat a completely restored nineteenth century stagecoach.

Some days we took tours. We rode in a bus several hours to Coba, the site of Mayan ruins that are just now being restored. There, we hiked a mile and a half into the jungle and watched an archaeologist measure and record a pyramid so high it poked above the treetops. The day before, we were told, they unearthed a vase more than one thousand years old. I bought a book in a grass hut on Mayan history for Laurel.

At Xcarte, we waded in a lagoon with tropical fish nibbling at our toes and knees and meandered through a lush butterfly pavilion, doggedly attempting to photograph a particular cobalt-blue one. At the marketplace in Tulum, we bartered for a nativity set for Karen and Rami with one of the dozens of teenage vendors who lured us in with the words, "Theez iz the place you are looking for, Señor."

And on the day we almost missed the boat, we explored Contoy. Eighteen miles off the coast of Cancun, the island of Contoy is one of the major nesting sites in the world for frigate birds. They have a wingspan of ninety inches, and the males inflate a large red pouch on their necks when courting. Only 150 visitors are allowed on the island each day.

If there has been one consistent element to our vacations, it has been David wearing a multipocketed bird-watching vest with a pair of binoculars to his eyes. The trip to Contoy was, to David, the highlight of our week; therefore, it was important to me. When our prearranged driver arrived an hour late, we frantically asked what had happened, but he spoke no English and didn't seem to comprehend our concern. He gestured us on board, took the seat behind the wheel, and we were off. For the hour-long ride to Cancun, we sat rigidly in our seats, glancing at our watches every few minutes.

Twenty minutes after the boat had been scheduled to leave, he pulled into a parking lot and spoke animatedly in Spanish with two men, all three of them pointing and gesturing. He jumped back on the bus without a word to us and, dodging in and out of traffic for a mile or so, pulled up abruptly beside a restaurant. He motioned for us to follow, and we did, on the run—through the restaurant, out a back door, down the length of a dock on a canal. We stood to the side while he engaged in another animated Spanish discussion with a woman in a boathouse, and then he turned and left without even a glance in our direction.

That's when she said to us in English, "Follow me," and we did. Weaving around cars in the crowded two-lane road, she said, "Lucky for you the tide was too high for the boat to get under the bridge at the end of the canal. I've radioed ahead, and we've got just enough time to make it."

Ten miles out to sea, the captain cut the engines and invited us to snorkel on a coral reef. We'd never tried snorkeling before, but how hard could it be? Everyone who vacations in the Caribbean snorkels. We donned flippers, life preservers, masks, breathing tubes, and jumped in when our language group was called.

The flippers served as anchors on my feet. The life preserver wasn't cinched tight enough and bobbed awkwardly around my chin and ears. I hyperventilated into the breathing tube and steamed up the mask. I could hear the English-speaking voices drifting farther and farther away, while in a panic, I dog paddled and thrashed twenty feet from the boat. Was anyone around? Who knew—I couldn't see through the steamed-up mask.

And then I heard David's exasperated voice. "I'm going back to the boat," he said. His mask wouldn't seal over his mustache and was filling up with water.

"Wait up!" I called, gasping, kicking, splashing, yet at the same time relieved I didn't have to admit I, too, was in trouble.

"Breathe slower, breathe slower." I heard the urgent command coming from the direction of the boat before one of the attendants grasped the strap of my life preserver, hauled my deadweight to the boat, and hoisted me on board. For the second time that day, David and I sat meekly in our seats, waiting for the attention directed toward us to die down.

"Your marriage is a work in process," a friend said to me recently. I had not thought of it in those words, but I had to agree. I am me, he is him, and these days, there is no push to conform or convert. Only an effort to understand and use our combined or individual talents to the best advantage of us as a couple. And that's what we went to Mexico to celebrate.

"What did you learn today?" I asked David on the boat ride back from Contoy. I expected him to speak of the birds he had seen: frigate, brown booby, the extremely rare red-footed booby, or the many facts of the Caribbean the naturalist had lectured about over the intercom.

"I learned," he said very seriously, "that we're not quite ready for snorkeling." And we laughed, long and loud and uncontrolled, in the middle of the sea, in the middle of the world, in the middle of a marriage very much in process.

Gathering

STILL

Sandra Doran

I was supposed to be writing this last chapter on an island. Not in my tiny home office, rain dripping outside, the sound of the "Discovery Channel" murmuring through the wall, two housebound kids sprawled out on the floor wrapped in blankets, husband in and out, asking if I've seen the extension cord lately. I'd pictured myself describing the context, the call of gulls, salt and spray splashing upward from rocks, a tugboat on the horizon. Instead, I will arise from the chair someone discarded on the side of the road two years ago and check the laundry in the midst of paragraphs, passing a sink-load of dishes on the way.

It's not that it was an exotic island. Truth be told, the last time I made the trip out, I gripped the sides of the ferry, ashen-faced, while the lurching seas drenched the back of my head with icy water and sent passengers retching to the sides of the boat, a fourth-grade girl using her lunchbox to catch her heaving. But the thought of island life enthralled me. "What are you doing this summer?" friends would ask. And I'd reply, "I'll be teaching a graduate course on Block Island every Monday and Tuesday for the first five weeks. I'll drive down to Point Judith on Monday morning, they'll put me up at a hotel on the island, and I'll be back Tuesday evening." I thought of two free days a week—no cooking, no cleaning, just uncluttered hours to think, write, plan my classes.

I was typing the last lines of the syllabus when the graduate department called. "I just got a call from the island," said the dean. "We're going to have to cancel. They can't get the numbers."

I went into somewhat of a panic at first. No class to teach. No island awaiting me. No paycheck for five weeks. A block of time I hadn't planned on, gaping open, ahead, unfilled, an air bubble in my gray matter that hadn't yet worked itself into my psychic space. I replaced the phone on its cradle, fired up the computer, began furiously typing e-mail messages. "I'm looking for freelance work," I in-putted. "I know it's last minute, but do you have anything?"

Nobody did.

By the next morning, the air bubble had begun to work itself out, the gray matter had begun to adjust to the idea that five unplanned weeks lay ahead, that money would be a scarcity, time a commodity. I went on with my life, writing appointments into my datebook as they inevitably arose, suddenly aware of my actions every Monday and Tuesday.

I wasn't supposed to be here, I thought, on the first Monday evening, seated with my family around the supper table, passing the Garden Burgers and insisting that Jeffrey eat four raw baby carrots out of the package when he refused the salad. I wasn't supposed to be here, I thought, as my husband rushed out of the house for a board meeting and Eric, Jr. called from his bedroom that he didn't understand the math assignment.

I felt as if I'd been given an unexpected gift, like George Bailey in the movie *It's a Wonderful Life,* hyperaware of the various roles I played, the ways my life took on layers of meaning in everyday actions. Cleaning up the dishes, I was acutely conscious of the extra pressure Eric, Sr. would have felt if he'd had to concoct a supper before running out to a board meeting, the frustration Eric, Jr. would have felt if he'd had to face linear equations alone. I decided, that first Monday, to mentally take note of all I wasn't supposed to be able to do, the places I wasn't supposed to be able to go, for the next five weeks.

As the rhythm of my life went on naturally, I found myself the following Monday taking the train into Boston for the first time in a year, ascending the stairs of Back Bay Station with throngs of 6:00 a.m. to 6:00 p.m. regulars, scrutinizing the "T" schedule, and heading back down another set of stairs onto the orange line, arriving on a street I'd never seen, walking three blocks past buckets of flowers, storefront luncheonettes, teenagers skipping school. I found the entrance to Massachusetts General Hospital exactly as she had described, located her office, sat down for two hours in the midst of papers piled high and books in stacks on the floor, while she shared with me ideas for creating a class designed to help classroom teachers develop a program for children who struggled to read.

I wasn't supposed to be here, I thought, eagerly taking notes, thankful that I had met her one week before at a meeting of the New England Branch of the Dyslexia Society, stimulated by her clear, sharp thinking. Later, I found my way to Quincy Market; sat on a bench in the sun eating a large slice of pizza covered with artichoke hearts, red peppers, and mushrooms; drinking a blueberry smoothie from a tall paper cup.

I wasn't supposed to be here, I thought, as I tossed the cup into a wire basket flanked by pigeons; strode past two Asian women ordering Belgian waffles from a Kiosk; arrived back at the station; sat on a circular stone bench carved with the words "Freedom is never granted; it is won. Justice is never given; it is exacted"; rode back to Attleboro to the rushing of trees by the train window; picked up my car beside the supermarket; passed Eric's school just in time to stop and offer him a ride as he walked up the hill, backpack bulging, trumpet case swinging from his hand.

On the third Monday I wasn't supposed to be around, Jeffrey invited me to a field day at his school. "Parents don't have to come," he said politely. "But it would be fun if you want to." I wanted to.

I stood in a relay line, sprinted to a large balloon, and sat down on it hard until it popped. I jumped, panting, in a burlap sack. I lobbed bean bags into a bucket. Won the water-balloon toss. Lost the jump-rope competition. Sank my teeth into watermelon. Sat on the grass beside Jeffrey against the wall below the windows to his classroom, arm encircled around his waist. I wasn't supposed to be here, I thought. I squeezed over a little closer to his spot on the grass. Not yet a teenager, he smiled up at me in gratitude and pleasure.

Looking ahead to the fourth Monday, I realized I had an anniversary coming up. Pulling out a free coupon I'd won last summer by writing an article about the hotel where we'd spent our honeymoon twenty-two years before, I reserved two nights. My parents agreed to take the children. Eric and I drove out to the Cape after church, our conversation relaxed and easy, marveling at the ability to establish a train of thought when every two words were not interrupted by "MOM, my lizards are out of crickets!" "DAD, this stupid printer is jammed!"

For two nights and three days, we flowed through the luxury of time, talked about things that mattered, drew close to one another in the place we had started our journey twenty-two years before. I wasn't supposed to be here, I thought, analyzing the nature of our relationship, our oneness, our individuality.

"Did you know," Eric asked, seated beside me in a sand chair, engrossed in *Nuts and Volts* magazine, "that in an electrical current the first electron never actually makes it to the end? They just vibrate, causing the last electron in place to be vibrated by the one before it . . ." We talked about scientific assumptions, the ways in which all of us form fourth-grade understandings and hold onto them for years, then we lapsed back into our reading.

"That's incredible," I punctuated the silence a few moments later. "Did you know that the same nervous system pathways that govern motor production govern speech production?" We talked about children, the connections between seemingly disparate acts, buttoning a sweater, pronouncing a word.

Later, we walked along the beach, scanning the tide line with its jagged string of broken shells, black strands of washed-up seaweed, rocks, brittle bits of crabs. Stooping, Eric picked up what appeared to be some type of dried sea-necklace, a brown-gold cord with flat ovals attached. Shaking it, he found that some tiny treasure awaited discovery inside. Eagerly, I split open a pod, poured a handful of tiny shells into Eric's palm, one-quarter the size of popcorn seeds, perfectly formed, whorled symmetrically into minuscule, exquisite shapes.

"How could this be?" we marveled. "What type of creature would produce this necklace of shells? Does this mean that shells are 'hatched' and grow up into the large, granddaddies that you place to your ear to hear the roar of the sea? Is this necklace a plant or an animal? Where did it come from?"

The necklace was carefully wrapped in tissue paper from the hotel, made its way back to Attleboro, intrigued the boys with its wonders.

Today, the fifth Monday, I sit at my computer, the necklace before me, a computer printout describing the "channeled whelk" beside it. "Channeled whelks live in the sand just below the level of the low tide," reads the *Assateague Naturalist*. "The females lay strings of egg capsules, attaching one end in the sand. Each capsule can hold up to 100 eggs, and a small hole at the top allows the larvae to escape. The channeled whelk is found from Massachusetts to northern Florida."

If anyone had told me that shells start out as tiny eggs laid in the sand and grow up into the large whelks I so delighted in finding as a child on a small island in Connecticut, I probably would have laughed derisively or at least demanded proof. But here before me is the evidence, the explanation.

Next Monday I will be immersed in teaching a graduate class, the start of Summer Two. I will have little time for discovering nature's wonders, checking references on sea creatures. But I suspect that I will be gathering still, amassing new layers of meaning like the channeled whelk, collecting insight, hope, richness, and knowledge along the way. For life to me will always be a horizontal gathering, a walk along the tides, a journey where scanning the shore for treasures holds as much importance as arriving at the high end of the dunes.

Gathering

A SENSE OF PLACE

Dale Slongwhite

"We could move if you want," David says. "You choose this time, and I'll follow."

I could move from this place where I never wanted to be? I could go anywhere? *My* choice? So I think. I meditate. I send for brochures, and I visit. I look at maps with eager sense of possibility. I picture my life somewhere else, and I feel excitement in the anticipation.

David accepted his current job in densely populated north-eastern Massachusetts nearly thirteen years ago on the day Hurricane Gloria hit. I remember standing in a neighbor's backyard in a suburban Connecticut town examining a gigantic fallen tree that had barely missed their house. Leaves littered their yard like confetti after a royal wedding. The air was ominously still, an invisible foe poised to smother us should nature send the order. Overhead, a gray sky affixed itself to the heavens like duct tape against brighter days.

"We're moving," David brightly told the neighbors. He beamed, a college-educated man proud to be leaving the cold, dusty warehouse for a position with promise. Good benefits. Respect. The one who had more to offer than any other candidate. Maybe he could move up. And I wanted that for him, too, but what about *me*? What about *us*? What about *the girls*? My heart stuck in my throat pulsating rapidly. My smile was a pasted-on hyphen. My feet . . . they made me hoist them up and plop them down each step on the walk home. My mood melded with the weather.

Two days after accepting the job, he left. On Sunday night, he took his rusted-out Honda with its falling-off parts and drove two hours north . . . into the city with its agitated motorists, bristling pavement, streetwise children, and hefty price tag . . . into a world we did not know we did not understand.

He left in his rearview mirror our little home where the children rode bikes in the street, built clubhouses in the backyard, walked to school, organized games with children who knew and loved them. A world I was able to juggle with a part-time job with flexible hours. A world that for us would be no more.

I packed. I packed and I cried. But when he came home on Friday night bubbling with the adventures of his week . . . about the professional people and the clean environment and the food in the cafeteria . . . I listened and I did not speak.

We moved into a three-room apartment on Main Street with a rent the same as the mortgage on our three-bedroom home on a circle off a side street. I worked full time, my can opener replacing my recipe box, a haze of doom replacing my dreams. We did not know for years the psychological wounds inflicted upon the girls by the dramatic change in our lifestyle.

But I can leave now. I can choose a place, and I can go.

It will have to be a place near the ocean, or I could not breathe. From where I live now, we have discovered a myriad of quaint little coastal towns less than an hour away. In Massachusetts, there's Newburyport with its boardwalk along the harbor, open air band concerts in summer, fireworks over the ocean on the Fourth of July, and the Plum Island bird refuge where David spotted the snowy owl. There's Rockport, with dozens of specialty shops built on a jetty into the harbor, Motif #1—the red boathouse hung with hundreds of lobster-pot markers that is photographed thousands of times each year. There's Wingaersheek Beach, where we collected sand dollars; there's Gloucester, with its pier from which we embarked on a whale watch.

In New Hampshire, there's Portsmouth, where we ate lunch last Sunday, the second warm day after a cold snowy winter. Slowly making our way through omelettes and homemade maple-swirled bread, we watched through the wall of windows as a brightly painted red tugboat pushed a massive oil barge through the mouth of the river, under the raised suspension bridge, and into the harbor. The day before, the *first* warm day after a cold snowy winter, we slept on boulders in Maine, high above waves dousing rocks, seagulls squawking overhead in protest, children dodging the attacking water yet screeching in delight when the ocean won.

I can leave now, but where I go can be no farther from the ocean than this.

In less than an hour in the other direction, I can be in Boston. I can navigate the subway system now with precision and without fear, or I can drive if I choose and actually find where I want to go. I have attended numerous author readings and book signings, taken a graduate level writing class at Harvard University, joined more than a million people on the streets for festivities on New Year's Eve, sat on the roof of the Museum of Science parking garage to watch fireworks over the Charles River. I have listened to the Boston Pops in Symphony Hall, rooted for the Red Sox in Fenway Park, chanted with the Celtics fans in the brand new Fleet Center, poked around familiar shops in Quincy Market, eaten with my daughters in an interior flower garden courtyard of the Isabella Stewart Gardner Museum on Mother's Day then gazed in awe at the 300-year-old original oil paintings displayed magnificently in upstairs galleries.

I can leave now, but where I go can have no less culture than this.

After living in the small apartment for several months, we began looking for a house. The technological age had invaded metropolitan Boston, driving home prices beyond our grasp. We were laughed out of real estate offices with what we thought was a sizable down payment. "Go north," they said, so we did. Town after town after town, until finally, one of the lesser-desired ones opened its arms and let us in. It is a city known as a mecca for drug dealers, a city whose public high school lost accreditation last year, a city with the second highest teen birth rate in the state of Massachusetts. In this city's furthermost northeastern corner, we found a large cape at the end of a dead-end street unscathed by the reputation of its hosting community. Every day for the last twelve years, David has battled twenty-five miles of snarling traffic. For half those years, the girls accompanied him to a private school near his place of employment.

At first our roof leaked, but now I am writing in a swath of light beamed in from a brand-new cranked-open skylight. At first the floor in the kitchen was a smoothed-away pattern of pea-green linoleum, but now it is a stretch of sleek Pergo the entire width of the house. At first the fireplace was shabby and rimmed in black, but now it is painted cream and stenciled with flowers. We have wallpapered between the beams in the living room so it looks like a tin ceiling. We have hung on the walls, going up the stairs, the 8-inch by 10-inch black-and-white photos I developed in the darkroom for a college class. Outside the picture window in the kitchen, David has mounted a windowbox in the shape of a boat that I hauled back from Cape Cod. At Christmas I fill it with red bows and pines we gather in the woods; in the spring, purple pansies; in the summer, a variety of annuals; in the fall, miniature gourds and pumpkins. We have painted and stenciled and wired in chosen light fixtures and planted flowers until now this place is ours.

I can go anywhere now, but it will have to be a place where I feel as comfortable as this.

I have lived here long enough to know the used-to-bes. "I took a right at the Den," I tell David, and he knows Boston Market is there now but it used to be the Den. "I'm going to Osco Drug," I say, "where the church used to be." There is a sense of belonging when you know the used-to-bes.

My doctor knows my family, and he knows my history. "Is this anything like the time back in '89?" he asks. We are in a small examining room, and he is professional and caring. Out in the hallway, his demeanor changes, and he grins a wide, almost boyish, grin. "How's Laurel doing?" he asks. "Boy, do we miss her. She was the glue that held this place together." For eight months before leaving for college, Laurel worked as a receptionist in his office. They know her. They care about her. They care about me.

But I can go now. Anytime I want. Any place I want. I could leave the grocery store where only long-timers like myself can find the canned french-fried onion rings. I could leave the mall where I know every corner of every favorite store and David knows I will always park in the second level behind Filenes. I could leave my relationships with people at church, in my neighborhood, at work. I could leave this place where I can finally decode the radio traffic reports . . . "backed up to the Braintree split . . . slows you down through the Sumner all the way to the gas tank." (It used to be the gas *tanks,* but they deflated one, and *that* was something to see.)

If I could do it over again, I would not come here. But I cannot do it over. I am here. It is from *this* spot, *this* moment in time, that I must decide where I will go next. And in spite of myself, I must admit that I am a different woman from the one who moved to this place nearly thirteen years ago. I am not who I wanted to be, not who I dreamed I would be. I am better. I am stronger. I know more . . . more about life, more about empathy, more about flexibility, more about the world of work, more about computers, more about what it takes to successfully navigate a life. And this place had a part in shaping who I have become. It is part of me. I am part of it.

I look at the girls. They are grown now, and with admirable inner strength, they have risen above those difficult early days. Karen

is excelling at Harvard University and Laurel at Mount Holyoke College. They are making choices. They are building lives for themselves.
They are also better. They are also stronger. I am proud of them.

I could go now, but for now, I think I would like to stay.